Guitar Chord Songbook

Love Songs

ISBN 978-1-4234-6803-5

7777 W. Bluemound Rd. P.O. Box 13819 Milwaukee, WI 53213

Visit Hal Leonard Online at
www.halleonard.com

Contents

All I Ask of You

from THE PHANTOM OF THE OPERA

Music by Andrew Lloyd Webber
Lyrics by Charles Hart
Additional Lyrics by Richard Stilgoe

Melody:

No more talk of dark-ness, for - get these wide-eyed fears.

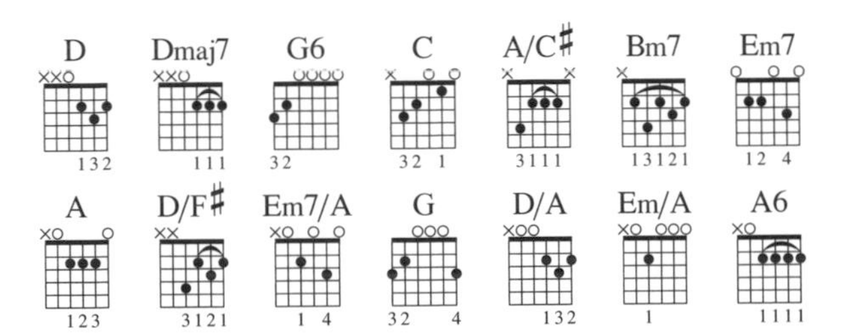

Verse 1

D
Raoul: No more talk of darkness, forget these wide-eyed fears.

Dmaj7 G6 C A/C♯
I'm here, nothing can harm you, my words will warm and calm you.

D
Let me be your freedom, let daylight dry your tears.

Dmaj7 G6 C A/C♯
I'm here, with you, be - side you, to guard you and to guide you.

Chorus 1

D Bm7 Em7 A
Christine: Say you love me ev'ry waking moment,

D/F♯ Bm7 Em7 Em7/A
Turn my head with talk of summertime.

D Bm7 Em7 A
Say you need me with you now and always.

D/F♯ G D/A
Promise me that all you say is true,

Em/A A6 Em/A D
That's all I ask of you.

Verse 2

D
Raoul: Let me be your shelter, let me be your light.

Dmaj7 G6 C A/C♯
You're safe, no one will find you, your fears are far be - hind you.

D
Christine: All I want is freedom, a world with no more night.

Dmaj7 G6 C A/C♯
And you, always be - side me, to hold me and to hide me.

Chorus 2

D Bm7 Em7 A
Raoul: Then say you'll share with me one love, one lifetime

D/F♯ Bm7 Em7 A
Let me lead you from your solitude.

D Bm7 Em7 A
Say you need me with you, here be - side you.

D/F♯ G D/A
Anywhere you go, let me go too.

Em7/A A6 Em7/A D
Christine, that's all I ask of you.

Chorus 3

D Bm7 Em7 A
Christine: Say you'll share with me one love, one lifetime.

D/F♯ Bm7 Em7 Em7/A
Say the word and I will follow you.

D Bm7 Em7 A
Share each day with me, each night, each morning.

D/F♯ G D/A
Say you love me. *Raoul:* You know I do.

Em7/A A6 Em7/A D
Christine & Raoul: Love me, that's all I ask of you.

Interlude

| D Bm7 | Em7 A | D/F♯ Bm7 |
| Em7 Em7/A | D Bm7 | Em7 A |

Outro

D/F♯ G D/A
Christine & Raoul: Anywhere you go, let me go too.

Em7/A A6 Em7/A D
Love me, that's all I ask of you.

And I Love Her

Words and Music by
John Lennon and Paul McCartney

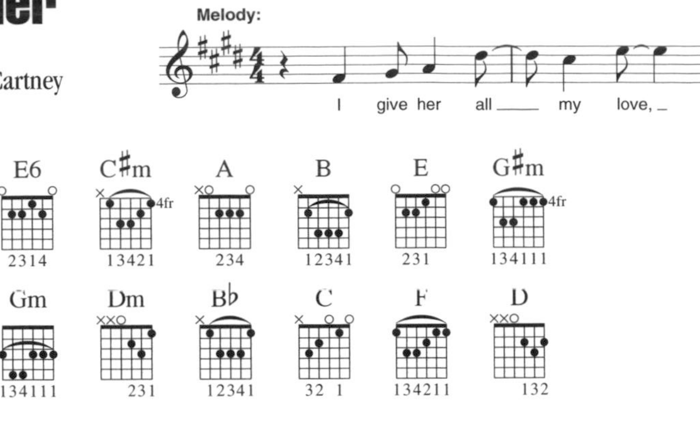

Intro | **F#m** | | **E6** | | |

Verse 1

F#m **C#m**
I give her all my love,

F#m **C#m**
That's all I do,

F#m **C#m**
And if you saw my love,

A **B**
You'd love her too,

E
I love her.

Verse 2

F#m **C#m**
She gives me everything,

F#m **C#m**
And tenderly,

F#m **C#m**
The kiss my lover brings,

A **B**
She brings to me,

E
And I love her.

Bridge

```
C♯m        B
  A love like ours
C♯m          G♯m
  Could never die
C♯m        G♯m
  As long as I
        B          B7
Have you near me.
```

Verse 3

```
F♯m            C♯m
  Bright are the stars that shine,
F♯m          C♯m
  Dark is the sky,
F♯m          C♯m
  I know this love of mine
A            B
  Will never die,
     E
And I love her.
```

Interlude

| **Gm** | **Dm** | **Gm** | **Dm** | **Gm** |
| **Dm** | **B♭** | **C** | **F** | |

Verse 4

```
Gm             Dm
  Bright are the stars that shine,
Gm           Dm
  Dark is the sky,
Gm           Dm
  I know this love of mine
B♭           C
  Will never die,
     F
And I love her.
```

Outro

| **Gm** | | **F** | | |
| **Gm** | | **D**

And I Love You So

Words and Music by Don McLean

(Capo 1st fret)

Intro |**Gmaj7** |**Am7** |**D7sus4** |**Gmaj7** |

Verse 1

```
Gmaj7               Am7
  And I love you ___ so.
C/D                  Gmaj7     Gmaj7/F#
  The people ask me ___ how,
Em  Em/D               Am7
          How I've lived 'till now.
C   Am7               D  Dsus2  D  Dsus2  D
  I tell them I don't know.
Gmaj7                  Am7
  I guess they under - stand
D7sus4  D7       Gmaj7           Gmaj7/F#
   How lonely life ___ has been.
Em                  Am7
  But life began again
C       C/D               Gmaj7  C/G
  The day you took my hand.
```

Chorus 1

```
Gmaj7      G+      G6       Gmaj7*
   And yes, ___ I ___ know

     Am7
How lonely life can be.

C/D
   The shadows follow me,

               Gmaj7          C/G          Gmaj7
An' the night ___ won't set ___ me free.

     Em    Em(maj7)/D#  Em/D  Gmaj7
But I don't let

     A7sus4      A7        A+
The evening get me down,

     Am7                      C/D    G
Now ___ that you're around ___ me.
```

Verse 2

```
Gmaj7            Am7
   And you love me too.

C/D                  Gmaj7      Gmaj7/F#
   Your thoughts are just for me.

Em   Em/D        Am7
       You set my spir - it free.

C      Am7           D7sus4  D7
   I'm happy that you do.

Gmaj7            Am7
   The book of life ___ is brief,

D7sus4  D7           Gmaj7        Gmaj7/F#
          And once a page ___ is read

Em          Am7
   All but life ___ is dead.

C  C/D         Gmaj7      C/G  Gmaj7  C/G
      That is my ___ belief.
```

Chorus 2

```
Gmaj7      G+      G6        Gmaj7*
   And yes, ___ I ___ know

      Am7
How lonely life can be.

     C/D
The shadows follow me,

               Gmaj7          C/G             Gmaj7
An' the night ___ won't set ___ me free.

     Em    Em(maj7)/D♯  Em/D  Gmaj7
But I don't let

     A7sus4      A7               A+
The evening get ___ me down,

Am7                        C/D  Gmaj7    C/G  Gmaj7  C/G  Gmaj7
Now that you're around __________ me.
```

Beautiful

Words and Music by Jim Brickman,
Jack Kugell and Jamie Jones

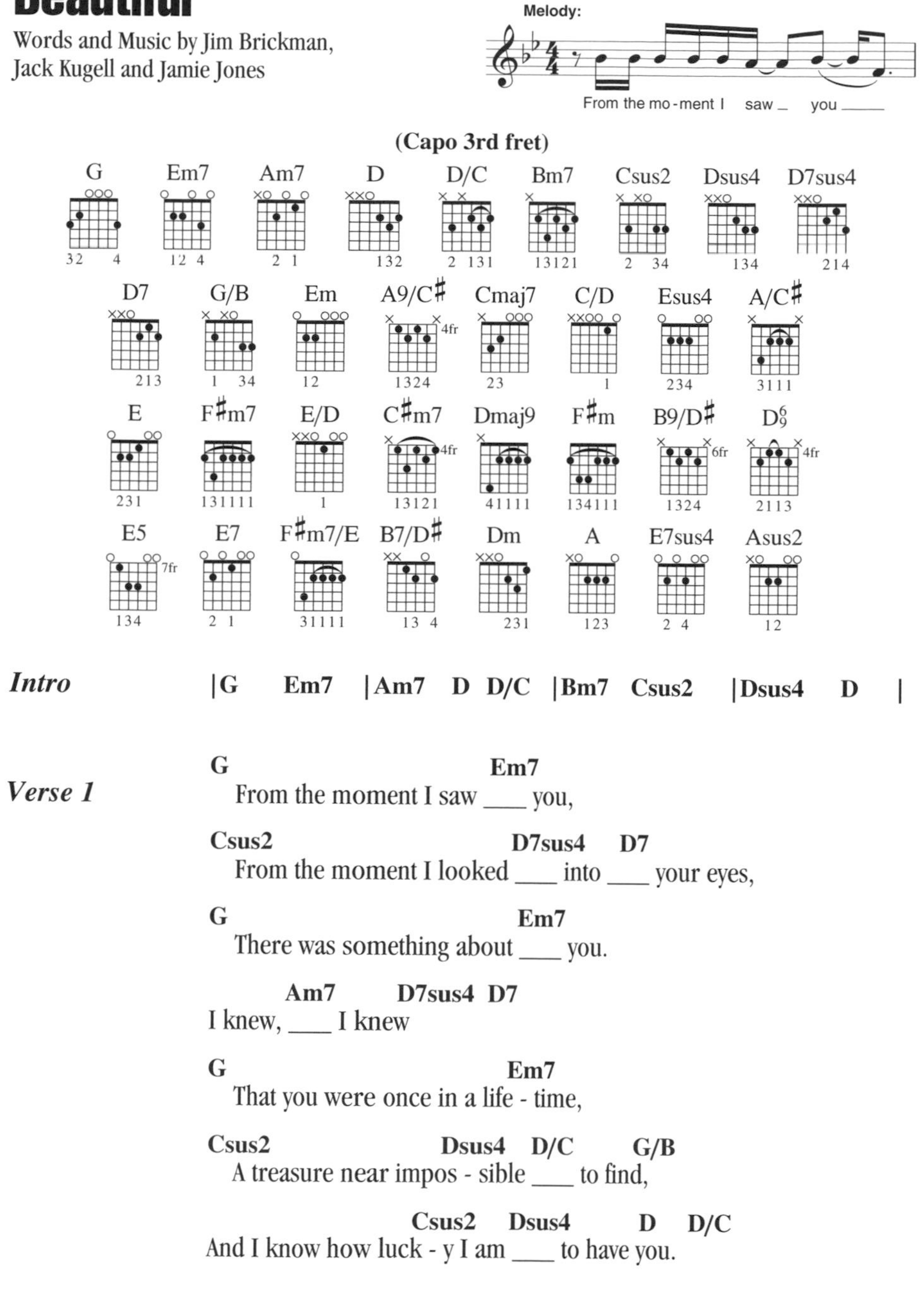

Intro

|G Em7 |Am7 D D/C |Bm7 Csus2 |Dsus4 D |

Verse 1

G Em7
From the moment I saw ___ you,

Csus2 D7sus4 D7
From the moment I looked ___ into ___ your eyes,

G Em7
There was something about ___ you.

Am7 D7sus4 D7
I knew, ___ I knew

G Em7
That you were once in a life - time,

Csus2 Dsus4 D/C G/B
A treasure near impos - sible ___ to find,

Csus2 Dsus4 D D/C
And I know how luck - y I am ___ to have you.

Chorus 1

G/B   Csus2   Dsus4   D D/C
'Cause I've seen rain - bows that could take your breath away,

G/B   Em7   Am7   Dsus4 D/C
The beauty of the setting sun that ends a perfect day.

G/B   Csus2   Em D   A9/C♯
And when it comes to shoot - ing stars, I've seen a few,

Am7   G/B   Cmaj7
But I've never seen anything

Dsus4 C/D   G   Em7 Am7 D7sus4 D7
As beautiful as ___ you.

Verse 2

G   Em7
Holding you in my ___ arms,

Csus2   D7sus4   D7
No one else's fit ___ so per - fectly.

G   Em7   Am7   D7sus4 D7
I could dance forev - er with you, ___ with you.

G   Em7
And at the stroke of mid - night,

Csus2   Dsus4   D/C   G/B
Please forgive me if ___ I can't ___ let go,

Csus2   Dsus4   D   D/C
'Cause I never dreamed ___ I'd find a Cinder - ella of my own.

Chorus 2

G/B   Csus2   Dsus4   D D/C
'Cause I've seen rain - bows that could take your breath away,

G/B   Em7   Am7   Dsus4 D/C
The beauty of the setting sun that ends a perfect day.

G/B   Csus2   Em D   A9/C♯
And when it comes to shoot - ing stars, I've seen a few,

Am7   G/B   Cmaj7
But I've never seen anything

Dsus4 C/D   G   Em7
As beautiful as ___ you.

Bridge

Am7 D D/C G/B Csus2
La, da, da, da, da, ___ da, da.

Dsus4 Esus4
Oh, oh, ___ oh.

Chorus 3

A/C# D Esus4 E
I've seen rain - bows that could take your breath away,

A/C# F#m7 Bm7 E E/D
The beauty of the set - ting sun that ends a perfect day.

C#m7 Dmaj9 F#m E B9/D#
And when it comes to shoot - ing stars, I've seen a few,

Bm7 A/C# D6/9 E5
But I've never seen any - thing,

E7 A/C# F#m7 F#m7/E
Oh ___ no, I've never seen anything

B7/D# Dm A F#m7 Bm7 E E/D
As beautiful as you.

Outro

A F#m7
From the moment I saw ___ you,

Bm7 Esus4 E7sus4 Asus2 A
From the moment I looked ___ into ___ your eyes.

Baby, I'm-A Want You

Words and Music by David Gates

Melody:

Ba - by, I'm - a want you.

Tune down 1/2 step:
(low to high) Eb-Ab-Db-Gb-Bb-Eb

Amaj7 (321, 4fr) Bm/A (321) D (132) A (123) Amaj7* (1113) D/C# (4 132) Bm7 (13121)

D/E (1121) C#m7 (13121, 4fr) E/D (121, 4fr) D* (341, 5fr) F#7 (324) F# (321) Gmaj7/A (4321)

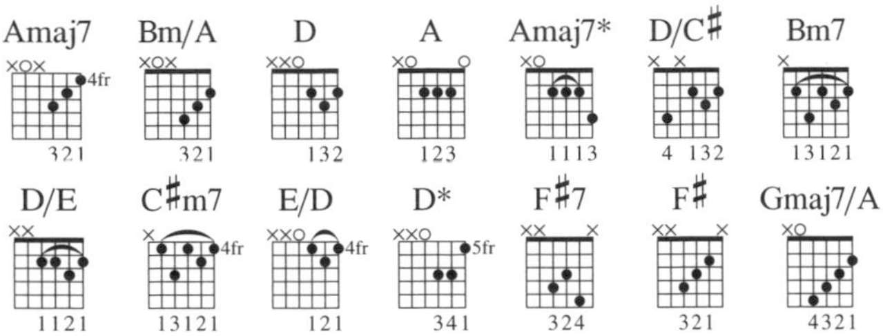

Intro |Amaj7 |Bm/A |Amaj7 |Bm/A D |

Verse 1

```
A                      Bm/A
Baby, I'm-a want you. Ba - by, I'm-a need you.
               Amaj7*                     D         D/C#
You're the on - ly one I care enough to hurt ___ about.
Bm7                         D/E
Maybe I'm-a crazy, but I just ___ can't live without your
```

Verse 2

```
   A                    Bm/A
Lov - in' and affection, giv - in' me direction,
            Amaj7*                                 D        D/C#
Like a guid - ing light to help me through my dark - est hour.
Bm7                             D/E                       A
Lately, I'm a-prayin' that you'll al - ways be a-stayin' beside ___ me.
```

```
               C#m7                                 E/D  D* D
Bridge 1       Used to be my life was just emotions pass - ing by,

               C#m7                                  E/D  D* D
               Feeling all the while and never really know - ing why.


Guitar Solo    |A         |Bm/A      |A         |D     D/C#  |
               Bm7                          D/E                   A
               Lately, I'm a-prayin' that you'll al - ways be a-stayin' beside ___ me.


               C#m7                                 E/D  D* D
Bridge 2       Used to be my life was just emotions pass - ing by.

               C#m7                                          E/D  D* D
               Then you came along and made me laugh and made me cry.

               F#7  F#    Bm7  D/E
               You  taught me  why.


                 A                      Bm/A
Verse 3        Ba - by, I'm-a want you. Ba - by, I'm-a need you.

               Amaj7*    Gmaj7/A
                 Oh, it took ___ so long to find you, baby.

                 A                      Bm/A                 A  Bm/A
               Ba - by, I'm-a want you. Ba - by, I'm-a need you.


Outro          ||: A       |Bm/A      |A        |Bm/A    :||  Repeat and fade
```

Beautiful in My Eyes

Words and Music by Joshua Kadison

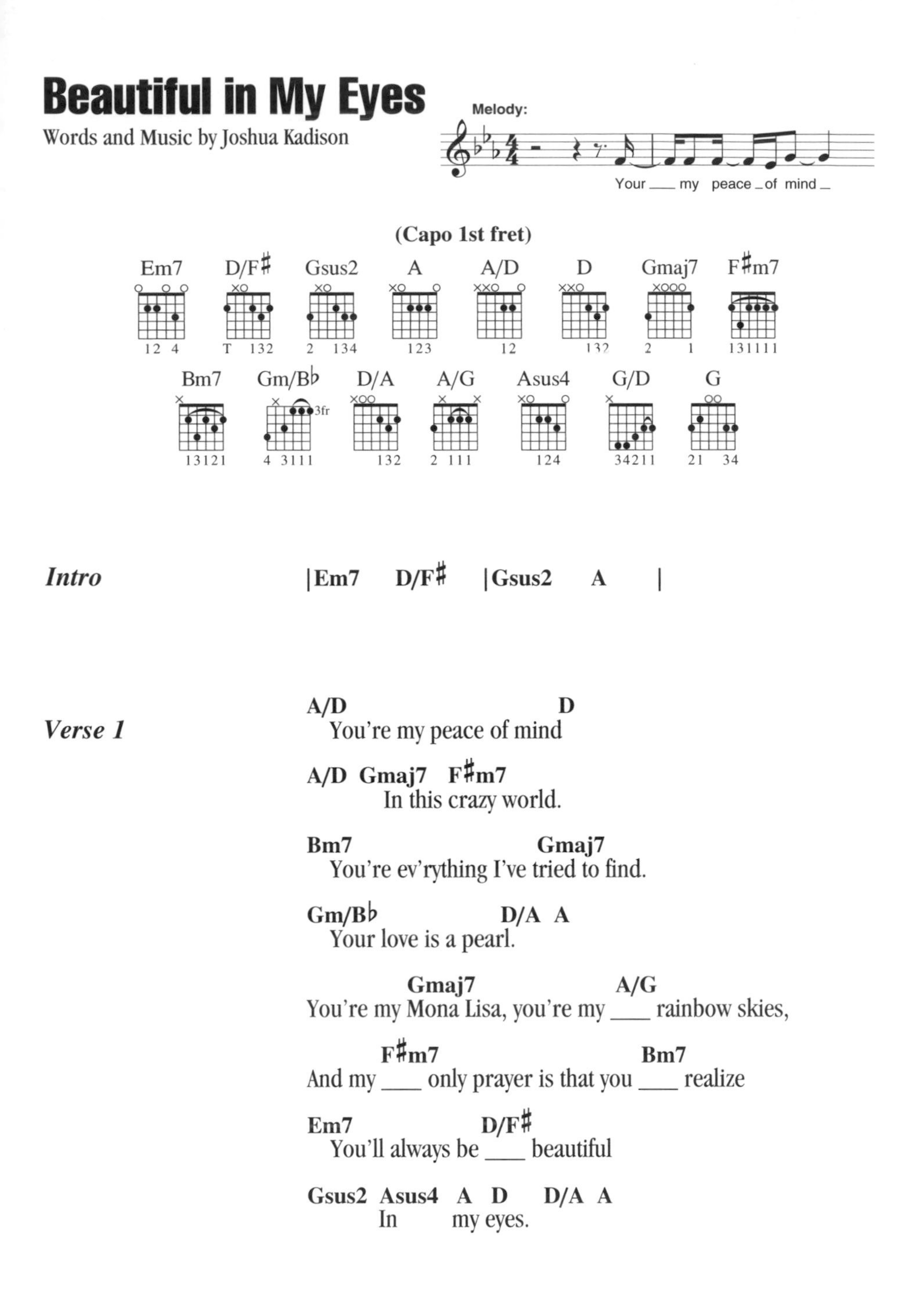

(Capo 1st fret)

Em7 D/F♯ Gsus2 A A/D D Gmaj7 F♯m7

Bm7 Gm/B♭ D/A A/G Asus4 G/D G

Intro |**Em7** **D/F♯** |**Gsus2** **A** |

Verse 1

A/D **D**
You're my peace of mind

A/D **Gmaj7** **F♯m7**
In this crazy world.

Bm7 **Gmaj7**
You're ev'rything I've tried to find.

Gm/B♭ **D/A** **A**
Your love is a pearl.

Gmaj7 **A/G**
You're my Mona Lisa, you're my ___ rainbow skies,

F♯m7 **Bm7**
And my ___ only prayer is that you ___ realize

Em7 **D/F♯**
You'll always be ___ beautiful

Gsus2 **Asus4** **A** **D** **D/A** **A**
In my eyes.

Verse 2

A/D D
The world will turn

A/D Gmaj7 F#m7
And the seasons will change,

Bm7 Gmaj7
And all the lessons we will learn

Gm/B♭ D/A A
Will be beautiful and strange.

Gmaj7 A/G
We'll have our ___ fill of tears, our share of sighs.

F#m7 Bm7
My only prayer is that you ___ realize

Em7 D/F#
You'll always be ___ beautiful

Gsus2 Asus4 A D
In my eyes.

Chorus 1

A D/A A D G/D
You will always be beautiful in my eyes.

D A G
And the passing years will show ___ that you will always grow

D/F# Em7 Asus4 A D Em7 D/F# Gsus2 A
Ever more ___ beautiful in my eyes.

```
                        A/D                     D
*Verse 3*    When there are lines upon my face

             A/D  Gmaj7     F#m7
                       From a lifetime of smiles,

             Bm7                        Gmaj7
               When the time comes to embrace

             Gm/Bb               D/A     A
               For one long last     while,

                     Gmaj7                   A/G
             We can laugh about how time ___ really flies.

                      F#m7                              Bm7
             We won't ___ say goodbye 'cause true love ___ never dies.

             Em7                D/F#
               You'll always be ___ beautiful

             Gsus2  Asus4  A   D
                     In        my eyes.
```

```
                        A  D/A  A                        D  G/D
*Chorus 2*   You will always be             beautiful in my eyes.

             D                                       A                     G
               And the passing years will show ___ that you will always grow

                       D/F#           Em7   Asus4  A   D
             Ever more ___ beautiful        in         my eyes.
```

```
                                            A                        G
*Outro*      The passing years will show ___ that you will always grow

                       D/F#            Em7   Asus4   A   D    Em7  D/F#  Gsus2  A  D
             Ever more ___ beautiful         in          my eyes.
```

(They Long to Be) Close to You

Lyric by Hal David
Music by Burt Bacharach

Melody:

Why do birds sud-den-ly ap - pear

(Capo 6th fret)

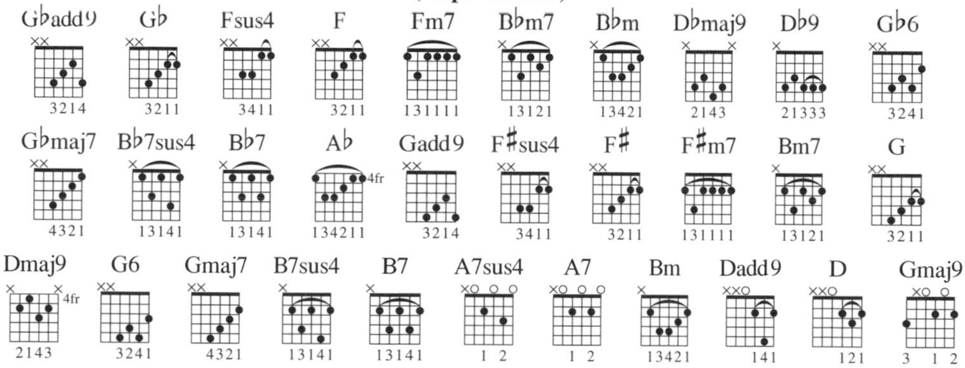

Gbadd9 3214 | Gb 3211 | Fsus4 3411 | F 3211 | Fm7 131111 | Bbm7 13121 | Bbm 13421 | Dbmaj9 2143 | Db9 21333 | Gb6 3241

Gbmaj7 4321 | Bb7sus4 13141 | Bb7 13141 | Ab 4fr 134211 | Gadd9 3214 | F#sus4 3411 | F# 3211 | F#m7 131111 | Bm7 13121 | G 3211

Dmaj9 4fr 2143 | G6 3241 | Gmaj7 4321 | B7sus4 13141 | B7 13141 | A7sus4 1 2 | A7 1 2 | Bm 13421 | Dadd9 141 | D 121 | Gmaj9 3 1 2

Intro

|Gbadd9 Gb |Gbadd9 Gb |Gbadd9 Gb |Gbadd9 |

Verse 1

Gbadd9 Fsus4 F
Why do birds suddenly ap - pear

Fm7 Bbm7 Bbm
Ev'ry time you are near?

Gb Gbadd9 Gb Gbadd9
Just like me, ______ they long to be

Dbmaj9
Close to you.

Gbadd9 Fsus4 F
Why do stars fall down from the sky

Fm7 Bbm7 Bbm
Ev'ry time you walk by?

Gb Gbadd9 Gb Gbadd9
Just like me, ______ they long to be

Dbmaj9 Db9
Close to you.

Bridge 1

```
Gb     Gb6    Gbmaj7  Gb6
On the day that you were born,

   Gb     Gb6    Gbmaj7
The angels got to - gether

Gb6        Fm7                         Bb7sus4  Bb7
  And de - cided to create a dream come ___ true.

       Gbadd9            Gb             Gbmaj7
So they sprinkled moon dust in your hair of gold

     Gb6                      Ab     N.C.
And starlight in your eyes of blue.
```

Verse 2

```
       Gbadd9           Fsus4  F
That is why all the girls in town

       Fm7          Bbm7  Bbm
Follow you all around.

Gb        Gbadd9  Gb        Gbadd9
Just like me, _____ they long to be

Dbmaj9     N.C.
Close to you.
```

Instrumental

```
|Gadd9     |F#sus4  F#  |F#m7    |Bm7        |
|Gadd9  G  |Gadd9    G  |Dmaj9   |           |
```

Bridge 2

```
G      G6      Gmaj7   G6
On the day that you were born,

   G      G6     Gmaj7
The angels got to - gether

G6          F#m7                         B7sus4   B7
   And de - cided to create a dream come ___ true.

        Gadd9             G              Gmaj7
So they sprinkled moon dust in your hair of gold

             G6            A7sus4  A7  N.C.
And starlight in your eyes of blue.
```

Verse 3

```
        Gadd9             F#sus4  F#
That is why all the girls in town

        F#m7         Bm7  Bm
Follow you all around.

G           Gadd9  G          Gadd9
Just like me, _____ they long to be

Dmaj9
Close to you.

G          Gadd9  G          Gadd9
Just like me, ____ they long to be

Dadd9    D  Dadd9  D  Dadd9  D  Dadd9
Close to you.
```

Outro

```
     Gmaj9  Dmaj9      D
||: Wah,    close to you.    :||  Repeat and fade
```

Butterfly Kisses

Words and Music by
Bob Carlisle and Randy Thomas

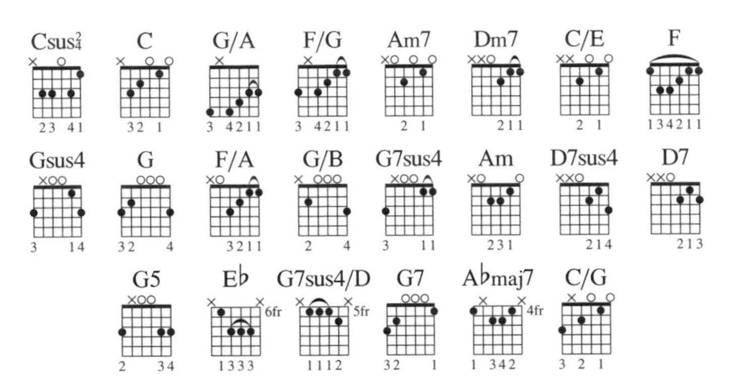

Intro

| Csus$^2_4$ C | Csus$^2_4$ C | Csus$^2_4$ C | Csus$^2_4$ C |
| Csus$^2_4$ C | Csus$^2_4$ C | Csus$^2_4$ C | G/A F/G |

Verse 1

C   Am7   C
  There's two things I know for sure,

Am7   C
She was sent here from heaven and she's daddy's little girl.

Dm7   C/E   F   Gsus4 G
As I drop to my knees ___ by her bed ___ at night,

Dm7   C/E   F   Gsus4
She talks to Je - sus, and I close my eyes,

G   F/A   G/B   C   F
  And I thank God for all ___ of the joy in my ___ life.

Chorus 1

G7sus4 Csus$^{2}_{4}$ C Csus$^{2}_{4}$ C
Oh, but most of all for butterfly kisses ___ after bedtime prayer,

Csus$^{2}_{4}$ C Csus$^{2}_{4}$ Am G
Stickin' little white flow - ers all up in her hair.

F C/E
"Walk beside the pony, Daddy, it's my first ride.

F C/E
I know the cake looks funny, Daddy, but I sure tried."

F/A G/B
Oh, with all that I've done wrong,

C D7sus4
I must have done something right

D7 F G5 Csus$^{2}_{4}$ C
To deserve a hug ev'ry morning and butterfly kisses at night.

| Csus$^{2}_{4}$ C | Csus$^{2}_{4}$ C | G/A F/G | C |

Verse 2

Am7 C
Sweet sixteen today,

Am7 C
She's looking like her momma a little more ev'ry day.

Dm7 C/E F Gsus4
One part wom - an, the oth - er part girl.

G Dm7 C/E F Gsus4 G
To perfume and make - up from ribbons and curls,

F/A G/B C F
Trying her wings ___ out in a great big world.

Chorus 2

                G7sus4 Csus2/4   C   Csus2/4   C
But I re - member butterfly kisses ___ after bedtime prayer,

             Csus2/4   C   Csus2/4   Am G
Stickin' little white flow - ers all up in her hair.

      F   C/E
"You know how much I love you, Daddy, but if you don't mind

     F   C/E
I'm only gonna to kiss you on the cheek this time."

           F/A   G/B
Oh, with all that I've done wrong

                     C   D7sus4
I must have done something right.

D7   F   G5   Csus2/4   C
  To deserve her love ev'ry morning and butterfly kisses at night.

Bridge

Csus2/4   C   Eb
  (All the precious time.)

G7sus4/D   Csus2/4   C   Csus2/4
  Oh, like the wind, the years ___ go by.

  C   Eb G7sus4/D F/A   Dm7   G7
(Precious butter - fly, ________ spread your wings and fly.)

Verse 3

Am7   C
She'll change her name today.

Am7   C
She'll make a promise, and I'll give her away.

Dm7   C/E   F   Gsus4
Standing in the bride ___ room just staring at her,

G   Dm7   C/E
  She asked me what I'm think - ing,

      F   Gsus4
And I said, "I'm not sure.

G   F/A   G/B   C   F
  I just feel like I'm losing my baby girl."

G7sus4 Csus$^{2}_{4}$ C Csus$^{2}_{4}$ C
Chorus 3 Then she leaned over, gave me butterfly kisses ___ with her momma there,

Csus$^{2}_{4}$ C Csus$^{2}_{4}$ Am G
Stickin' little white flow - ers all up in her hair.

F C/E
"Walk me down the aisle, Daddy, it's just about time.

F C/E
Does my wedding gown look pretty, Daddy? Daddy, don't cry."

F/A G/B
Oh, with all I've done wrong,

C D7sus4
I must have done something right

D7 F G7sus4
To deserve her love ev'ry morning and butterfly kisses.

F/A G/B
I couldn't ask God for more. Man, this is what love is.

A♭maj7 C/G
I know I've gotta let her go, but I'll always remember

F G7sus4 Csus$^{2}_{4}$ C
Ev'ry hug in the morning and butterfly kisses.

| Csus$^{2}_{4}$ C | Csus$^{2}_{4}$ C | G/A F/G | C ‖

Can't Help Falling in Love
from the Paramount Picture BLUE HAWAII

Words and Music by George David Weiss,
Hugo Peretti and Luigi Creatore

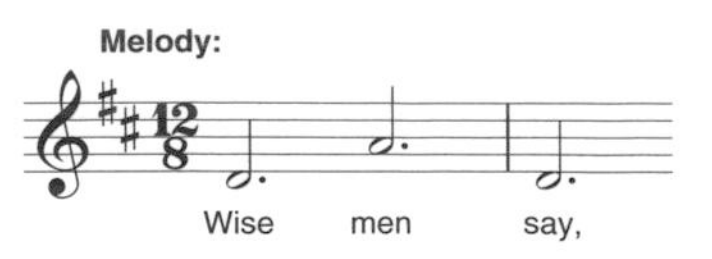

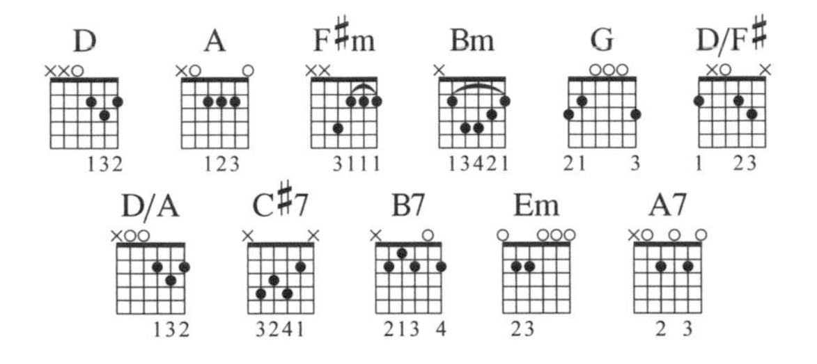

Intro | **D A** | **D** |

Verse 1

D F♯m Bm G D/F♯ A
Wise men say, only fools rush in.

G A Bm G D/A A D
But I can't help falling in love with you.

Verse 2

D F♯m Bm
Shall I stay?

G D/F♯ A
Would it be a sin

G A Bm G D/A A D
If I can't help falling in love with you?

Bridge 1

```
F#m         C#7  F#m         C#7
Like a river flows surely to the sea,
F#m          C#7
Darling, so it goes.
F#m         B7              Em  A7
Some things    are meant to be.
```

Verse 3

```
D    F#m Bm            G     D/F# A
Take my    hand, take my whole life,   too.
    G A    Bm  G         D/A A    D
For I  can't help falling in love with you.
```

Bridge 2

Repeat Bridge 1

Verse 4

```
D    F#m Bm            G     D/F# A
Take my    hand, take my whole life,   too.
    G A    Bm  G         D/A A    D
For I  can't help falling in love with you.
    G A    Bm  G         D/A A    D
For I  can't help falling in love with you.
```

The Colour of My Love

Words and Music by
David Foster and Arthur Janov

Melody:

I'll paint my mood in shades of blue, __

(Capo 1st fret)

C/G Fmaj7/A C F/A C/E Am7 Gsus4 G Cadd9

Fmaj7 Gadd9 G#°7 Am(add9) G6 Em7 Dm7 F/G G7sus4

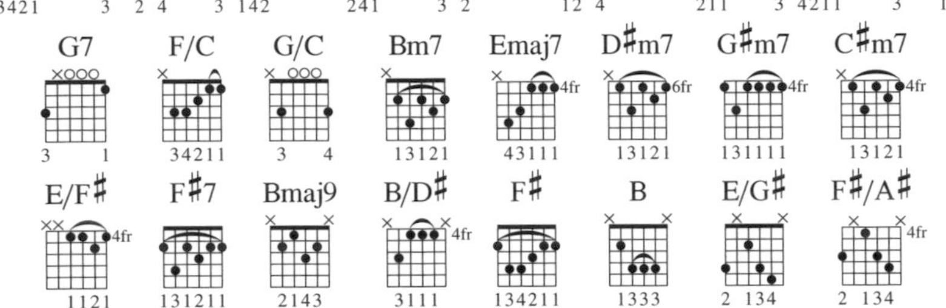

Intro	**|C/G Fmaj7/A |C/G Fmaj7/A |C F/A |C/E Am7 Gsus4 G |**

Verse 1

Cadd9 Fmaj7 Gadd9
I'll paint my mood in shades of blue,

G#°7 Am(add9)
Paint my soul to be with you.

G6 Fmaj7 Em7
I'll sketch my lips ___ in shadowed tones,

Am7 Dm7
Draw your mouth to my own.

Verse 2

Cadd9 Fmaj7 Gadd9
I'll draw your arms around my waist,

G♯°7 Am(add9)
Then all doubt I shall erase.

G6 Fmaj7 Em7
I'll paint the rain ___ that softly lands

Am7 F/G
On your windblown hair.

Verse 3

Dm7 Gadd9
I'll trace a hand to wipe your tears,

Em7 Am7
A look to calm your fears,

Dm7 Em7
A silhouette of dark and light

Fmaj7 G7sus4 G7 C
While we hold each other, oh, so _____ tight.

Verse 4

Fmaj7
I'll paint a sun to warm your heart,

Em7 Am7
Swearing that we'll ___ never part.

Dm7 G7sus4 G7 Cadd9
That's the color of ___ my love.

C/E Fmaj7
I'll paint the truth, ___ show how I feel,

Em7 Am7
Try to make you ___ completely real.

Dm7 Em7
I'll use a brush so light and fine

Fmaj7 G7sus4 G7 C F/C G/C
To draw you close and make you ___ mine.

Verse 5

```
C       Bm7    Emaj7
   I'll paint a sun to warm your heart,

                        D#m7               G#m7
Swearing that we'll ___ never, ever ___ part.

C#m7         E/F#    F#7      Bmaj9
   That's the color of ___ my love.

   B/D#      Emaj7
I'll draw the years all passing by,

                D#m7                G#m7
So much to learn, so much to try.

                  C#m7                D#m7
And with this ring our lives will start,

C#m7                        D#m7
   Swearing that we'll nev - er part.

C#m7                     D#m7
   I offer what you can - not buy,

     Emaj7            E/F#  F#   B  E/G#
De - voted love un - til      we die.

B  E/G#    B   E/G#  F#/A#  B
      Ooh, ___     ooh.
```

Feelings (¿Dime?)

English Words and Music by
Morris Albert and Louis Gaste
Spanish Words by Thomas Fundora

Melody:

Feel - ings, noth-ing

Am7 D7 G Em7 F#m7 B7 Em A7
Em(maj7)/D# Em7/D A F E7 Cmaj7 Bm7 D7b9

Intro

Am7	D7	G	Em7
Am7	D7	G	F#m7 B7
Em	A7	Em	A7

Verse 1

```
Em          Em(maj7)/D#  Em7/D
   Feelings,    nothing      more than feelings,

A          Am7          D7          G
   Trying to forget my     feelings of love.

   F#m7  B7
Of love.
```

Verse 2

```
Em           Em(maj7)/D#  Em7/D
   Teardrops     rolling down ___ on my face,

A             Am7           D7          G          F  E7
   Trying to ___ forget my     feelings ___ of love.
```

Chorus 1

```
Cmaj7      Am7   D7              Bm7
  Feelings,   for ___ all my life ___ I'll feel it.

E7          Am7
  I wish I never met you, girl;

D7                      F#m7                       B7
  You'll never come ___ this way, this way again.
```

Verse 3

```
Em       Em(maj7)/D#      Em7/D
  Feel - ings, feelings like I never lost you,

A                       Am7                    D7    G               F  E7
  And feelings like I'll ___ never have you    a - gain in my arms.
```

Chorus 2

```
Cmaj7      Am7   D7              Bm7
  Feelings,   for ___ all my life ___ I'll feel it.

E7             Am7
  I wish I nev - er met you, girl;

D7                    Bm7           E7
  You'll never come    this way again.
```

Chorus 3

```
Cmaj7  Am7      D7
Feelings,    whoa, whoa, whoa,

Bm7     E7
Feelings,    whoa, whoa, whoa,

Am7       D7       F#m7                 B7
  Feel you    again ___ in my arms. ___ Whoa.
```

Verse 4

```
Em          Em(maj7)/D#                  Em7/D
  Feelings, _________ feelings like I never lost you,

A                 Am7                     D7         G               F  E7
  And feelings like I'll never have you ___ again ___ in my life.
```

Chorus 4

```
Cmaj7     Am7   D7
   Feelings,    oh, ___ oh, oh,

Bm7           E7
     Feelings,     whoa, whoa, whoa,

Am7       D7             G
   Feel you     again in ___ my arms.

              F                    E7
Within my love, within my arms again.
```

Chorus 5

```
Cmaj7     Am7      D7
   Feelings,    whoa, whoa.

Bm7     E7
Feelings,    oh, oh.

Am7     D7♭9                 G  F♯m7  B7
Feel you     again in my arms.
```

Outro

‖: **Em** | **A7** :‖ ***Repeat and fade w/vocal ad lib.***

Could I Have This Dance

from URBAN COWBOY

Words and Music by Wayland Holyfield
and Bob House

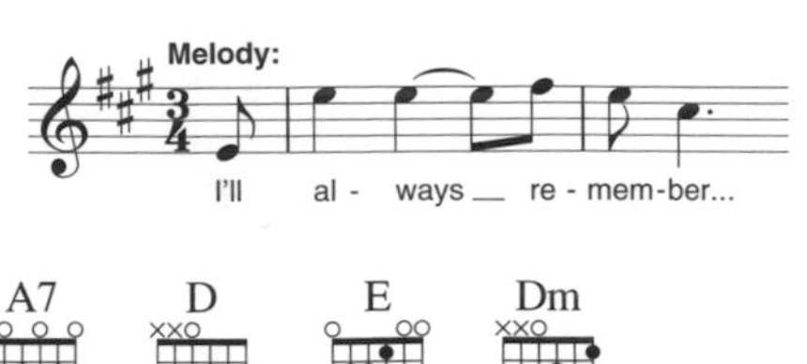

A Bm11/A Bm7 D/E A7 D E Dm

Intro | A | Bm11/A | Bm7 | D/E |

```
               A            A7
Verse 1        I'll always re-member

                 D                  E
               The song they were playing

                 D             E              A       D/E
               The first time we danced and I knew.

                   A               A7
               As we swayed to the music

                 D              E
               And held to each other,

               D    E      A
               I fell in love with you.


                   A          A7           D
Chorus 1       Could I have this dance for the rest of my life?

                   E                     D   E
               Would you be my partner ev'ry night?

               A             A7     D        Dm
               When we're to-gether it feels so right.

                   A                        E       A
               Could I have this dance for the rest of my life?
```

```
            A           A7
Verse 2     I'll always re-member

            D         E
            That magic moment,

                D           E        A   D/E
            When I held you close to me.

                A          A7     D          E
            As we moved to-gether, I knew for-ever

            D           E   A
            You're all I'll ever need.


Chorus 2    *Repeat Chorus 1*


                A          A7           D
Chorus 3    Could I have this dance for the rest of my life?

                 E                  D  E
            Would you be my partner ev'ry night?

            A             A7     D      Dm
            When we're to-gether it feels so right.

                A                   E
            Could I have this dance for the rest of my


Outro       | A         | Bm11/A    | Bm7       |
              life?

            | D/E     E | A         |
```

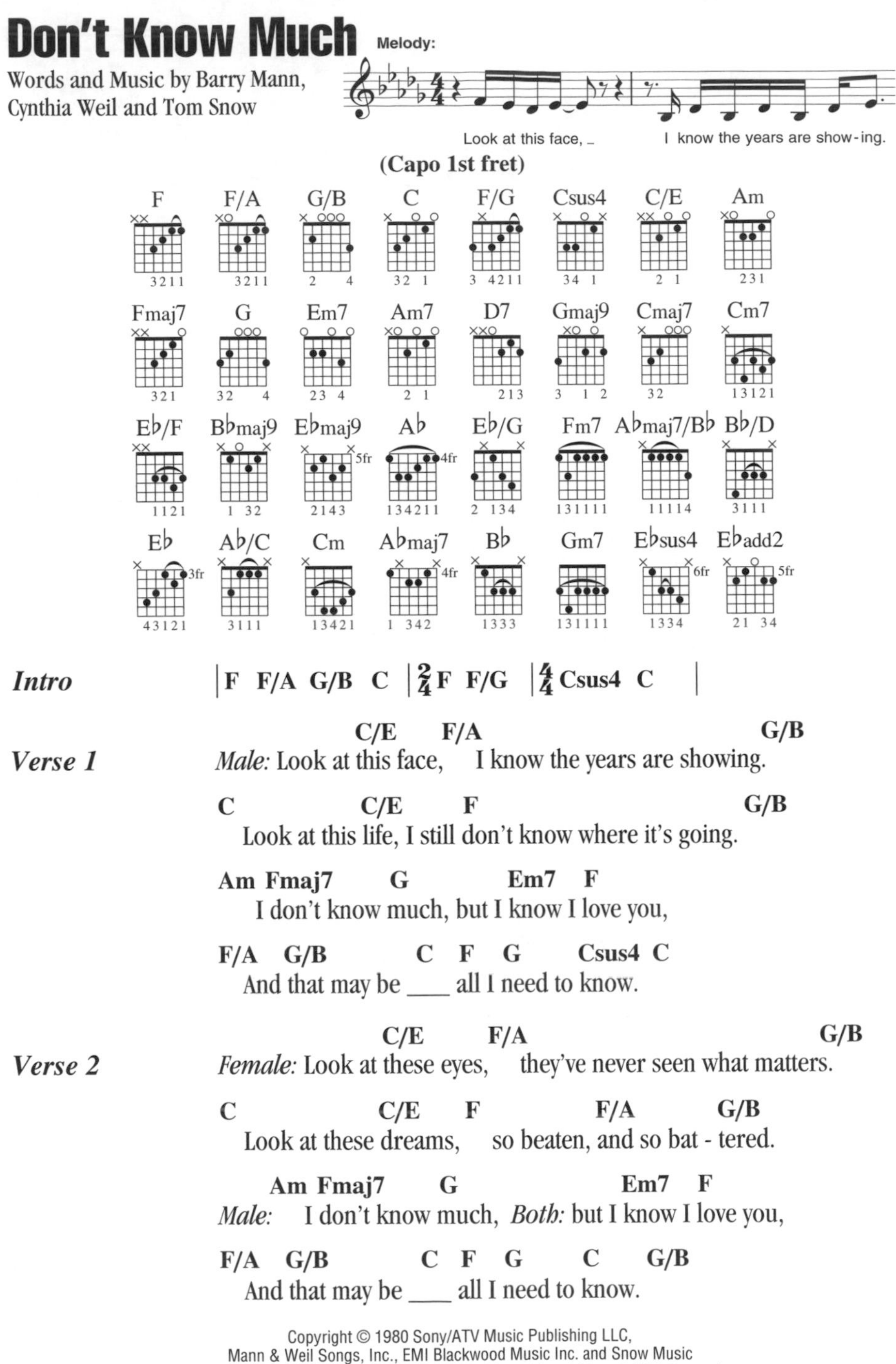

Don't Know Much

Words and Music by Barry Mann, Cynthia Weil and Tom Snow

Intro

| F F/A G/B C | 2/4 F F/G | 4/4 Csus4 C |

Verse 1

C/E F/A G/B
Male: Look at this face, I know the years are showing.

C C/E F G/B
Look at this life, I still don't know where it's going.

Am Fmaj7 G Em7 F
I don't know much, but I know I love you,

F/A G/B C F G Csus4 C
And that may be ___ all I need to know.

Verse 2

C/E F/A G/B
Female: Look at these eyes, they've never seen what matters.

C C/E F F/A G/B
Look at these dreams, so beaten, and so bat - tered.

Am Fmaj7 G Em7 F
Male: I don't know much, *Both:* but I know I love you,

F/A G/B C F G C G/B
And that may be ___ all I need to know.

Bridge

Am7 D7 Gmaj9 Cmaj7
Male: So many questions still left unan - swered.

F F/G C
So much I've never broken through.

Cm7 E♭/F B♭maj9 E♭maj9
Female: But when I feel you near me sometimes I see so clearly.

A♭ E♭/G Fm7
Both: The only truth I've ever known

E♭/G A♭maj7/B♭ B♭/D
Is me and you.

Verse 3

E♭ E♭/G A♭/C B♭/D
Male: Look at this man, so blessed with inspiration.

E♭ E♭/G A♭ A♭/C B♭/D
Both: Look at this soul, *Male:* still searching for salvation.

Cm A♭maj7 B♭ Gm7 A♭
Both: I don't know much, but I know I love you,

A♭/C B♭/D E♭ A♭maj7 B♭ E♭
And that may be ___ all I need to know.

Guitar Solo

| E♭ E♭/G | A♭ B♭ | E♭ E♭/G | A♭ A♭/C B♭/D |

Outro

Cm A♭maj7 B♭ Gm7 A♭
Both: I don't know much, but I know I love you,

A♭/C B♭/D E♭ A♭maj7 B♭ E♭ B♭/D
And that may be ___ all I need to know.

Cm A♭maj7 B♭ Gm7 A♭
I don't know much, but I know I love you,

A♭/C B♭/D E♭ A♭maj7 B♭ E♭sus4 E♭add2
And that may be ___ all there is to know. *Male:* Whoa.

Fields of Gold

Music and Lyrics by Sting

Bm7 G D G/B Asus4 Gsus2

13121 21 34 132 1 3 113 2 13

```
Intro      ‖: Bm7          |             :‖ Play 4 times

                  Bm7                     G
Verse 1    You'll re-member me when the west wind moves
                                  D
           Upon the fields of bar - ley.
                   Bm7                 G       D
           You'll for-get the sun in his jealous sky
                 G/B      Asus4    D
           As we walk in fields of gold.
           | Bm7        |     Gsus2| D          |           |
                 Bm7                   G
           So she took her love for to gaze a while
                                  D
           Upon the fields of bar - ley.
                Bm7                  G           D
           In his arms she fell as her hair came down
                 G/B        Asus4    D
           Among ___ the fields of gold.
```

Verse 2

```
          Bm7                  G
Will you stay with me, will you be my love
                          D
Among the fields of bar - ley?
          Bm7              G      D
We'll for-get the sun in his jealous sky
      G/B   Asus4  D
As we lie in fields of gold.
|Bm7       |     Gsus2| D        |        |
        Bm7                  G
See the west wind move like a lover so
                       D
Upon the fields of bar - ley.
         Bm7                 G      D
Feel her body rise when you kiss her mouth
       G/B      Asus4   D
Among ___ the fields of gold.
```

Bridge

```
Gsus2            D
  I never made promises lightly
Gsus2                      D
  And there have been some that I've broken,
Gsus2                 D
  But I swear in the days still left
            G/B     Asus4   D
We'll walk ___ in fields of gold.
      G/B     Asus4   D
We'll walk in fields of gold.
```

Guitar Solo

```
|Bm7      |G        |            |D         |
|Bm7      |G    D   |G/B Asus4   |D         |
```

Verse 3

```
          Bm7                           G
Many years have passed since those __ summer days
                              D
Among the fields of bar - ley.
         Bm7                 G        D
See the children run as the sun goes down
        G/B     Asus4   D
Among ___ the fields of gold.
            Bm7                  G
You'll re-member me when the west wind moves
                          D
Upon the fields of bar - ley.
            Bm7              G        D
You can tell the sun in his jealous sky
D            G/B      Asus4   D
When we walked in fields of gold.
             G/B      Asus4   D
When we walked in fields of gold,
             G/B      Asus4   D
When we walked in fields of gold.
```

Outro

```
||: D     Gsus2  D   :|| Play 7 times
| D                   |
```

Here and Now

Words and Music by
Terry Steele and David Elliot

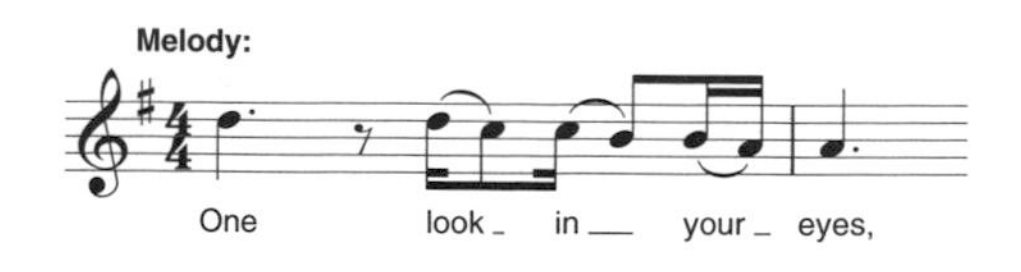

Cadd9 D7sus4 G D/G G/B F♯m7♭5 B7♭9
Em7 D Cmaj7 Bm7 Cm/E♭ G/D D♯°7
B7sus4 D/C D/F♯ G7sus4 Gadd2 B♭maj7 Fmaj7

Intro

```
| Cadd9  D7sus4 | G  D/G  G  G/B | Cadd9  D7sus4 |
```

Verse 1

```
G                 F♯m7♭5 B7♭9    Em7  D
One look in your eyes, and there I see

Cadd9        D7sus4     G
Just what you mean to me.

       D/G  G      F♯m7♭5    B7♭9  Cmaj7  Bm7
Here ___  in my heart         I believe

Cadd9        Cm/E♭  G/D  Cadd9
Your love is all _______ I  ever need.

                  G/B  D♯°7     Em7
Holding you close through the night,

       Cmaj7  D7sus4
I need you.    Yeah.
```

Verse 2

```
G                F#m7b5  B7b9    Em7 D
I look in your eyes and  there I see

      Cadd9    D7sus4    G
What happiness really means.

D/G         G           F#m7b5 B7b9      Cmaj7  Bm7
   The love ___ that we share     makes life so sweet.

     Cadd9       Cm/Eb G/D Cadd9
To - gether we'll always ____ be.

                 G/B D#°7 Em7
This pledge of love  feels   so right,

                   Cmaj7
And, ooh, I need you.
```

Chorus 1

```
F#m7b5  B7sus4      Cmaj7 D/C              D/F#   G  D/F#
              Here and now, I   promise to love faithfully.

Cmaj7          F#m7b5
You're all I need.

B7sus4      Cmaj7 D/C              D/F#  G    D/F#  Cadd9
   Here and now, I   vow to be one with   thee.

               D7sus4       G         D/G  G  G/B  Cadd9  D7sus4
Your love is all (I need.) ___ I need.

   G  D/G  G  G/B  Cadd9  D7sus4
Stay.
```

Verse 3

```
      G                 F#m7b5  B7b9     Em7  D
When I look in your eyes        there I see

Cadd9   D7sus4          G
All that a love should real - ly be.

                  F#m7b5  B7b9         Cmaj7  Bm7
And I need you more and more each day.

Em7          Cm/Eb  G/D Cadd9
Nothing can take       your love away.

                G/B  D#°7   Em7            Cmaj7
More than I dare ____ to dream, I need you.
```

Chorus 2

F♯m7♭5 B7sus4 Cmaj7 D/C D/F♯ G D/F♯
Here and now, I promise to love faithfully.

Cmaj7 F♯m7♭5
You're all I need.

B7sus4 Cmaj7 D/C D/F♯ G D/F♯ Cadd9
Here and now, I vow to be one with thee.

D7sus4
Your love is all I need.

Bridge

Cmaj7 D/C
(Starting here.) Ooh, and I'm starting now.

G Cmaj7
I believe. ___ (Starting here.)

I'm starting right here. (Starting now.)

D7sus4
Right now because I believe ___ in your love,

G7sus4
So I'm glad to take the vow.

Chorus 3

Cmaj7 D/C D/F♯ G D/F♯
Here and now, oh, I promise to love faithfully.

Cmaj7 F♯m7♭5
You're all I need.

B7sus4 Cmaj7 D/C D/F♯ G D/F♯ Cadd9
Here and now, I vow to be one with thee.

D7sus4
Your love ___ is all I

Outro

Gadd2 Cmaj7
‖: Need. I yeah, yeah. Uh, yeah.

B♭maj7 Cmaj7 Fmaj7
Ay ah, ___ love is all I :‖

Gadd2 Cmaj7
Need. I yeah, yeah. Uh, yeah.

B♭maj7 Cadd9 Gadd2
Ay ah, ___ yeah.

For All We Know

from the Motion Picture LOVERS AND OTHER STRANGERS

Words by Robb Wilson and Arthur James
Music by Fred Karlin

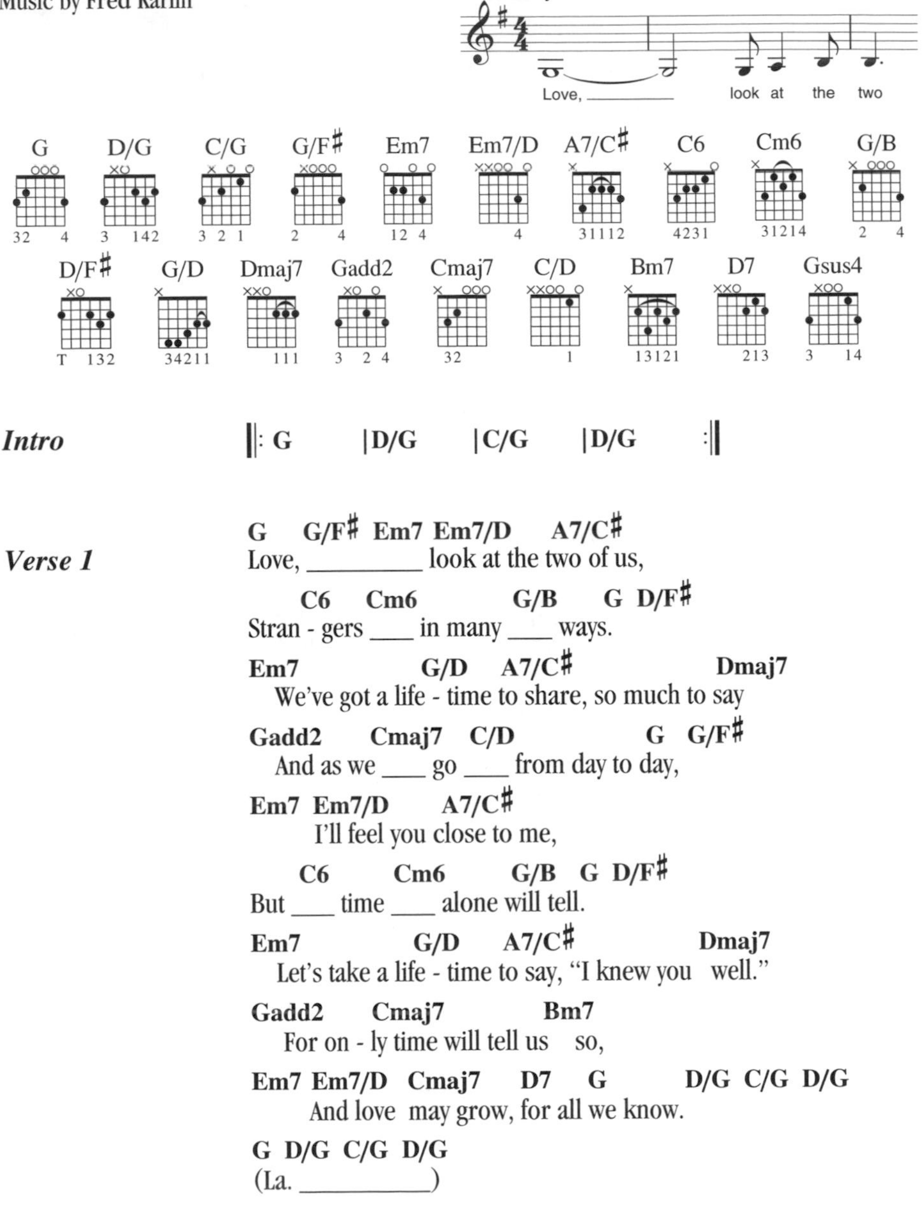

Intro

```
||: G      |D/G     |C/G     |D/G     :||
```

Verse 1

```
G    G/F♯  Em7  Em7/D      A7/C♯
Love, _________ look at the two of us,

     C6    Cm6            G/B      G  D/F♯
Stran - gers ___ in many ___ ways.

Em7              G/D    A7/C♯                 Dmaj7
  We've got a life - time to share, so much to say

Gadd2       Cmaj7   C/D                G   G/F♯
  And as we ___ go ___ from day to day,

Em7  Em7/D      A7/C♯
       I'll feel you close to me,

     C6       Cm6       G/B   G  D/F♯
But ___ time ___ alone will tell.

Em7              G/D     A7/C♯               Dmaj7
  Let's take a life - time to say, "I knew you   well."

Gadd2       Cmaj7          Bm7
  For on - ly time will tell us    so,

Em7  Em7/D  Cmaj7     D7    G           D/G  C/G  D/G
       And love  may grow, for all we know.

G  D/G  C/G  D/G
(La. __________)
```

Verse 2

```
G    G/F#  Em7 Em7/D    A7/C#
Love, _________ look at the two of us,

       C6    Cm6           G/B      G  D/F#
Stran - gers ____ in many ____ ways.

Em7                G/D    A7/C#              Dmaj7
   Let's take a life - time to say, "I knew you   well."

Gadd2      Cmaj7               Bm7
    For on - ly time will tell us   so,

Em7 Em7/D Cmaj7      D7    G          D/G  C/G  D/G
       And love   may grow, for all we know.

G  D/G  C/G  D/G  Gsus4  G
(La. __________)
```

Glory of Love

Theme from KARATE KID PART II

Words and Music by David Foster,
Peter Cetera and Diane Nini

Melody:

To - night_ it's ver - y clear,

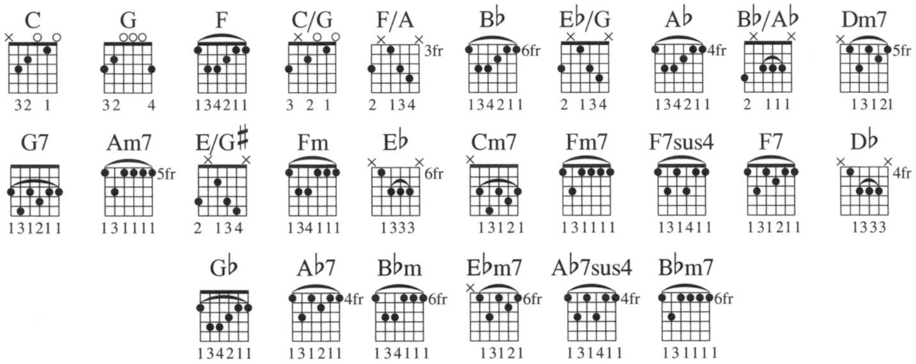

C (32 1) · G (32 4) · F (134211) · C/G (3 2 1) · F/A 3fr (2 134) · B♭ 6fr (134211) · E♭/G (2 134) · A♭ 4fr (134211) · B♭/A♭ (2 111) · Dm7 5fr (13121)

G7 (131211) · Am7 5fr (131111) · E/G♯ (2 134) · Fm (134111) · E♭ 6fr (1333) · Cm7 (13121) · Fm7 (131111) · F7sus4 (131411) · F7 (131211) · D♭ 4fr (1333)

G♭ (134211) · A♭7 4fr (131211) · B♭m 6fr (134111) · E♭m7 6fr (13121) · A♭7sus4 4fr (131411) · B♭m7 6fr (131111)

Verse 1

```
C
Tonight it's very clear,
G
As we're both standing here,
C           F            C/G   G
There's so many things I want to say.
C             F/A
I will always love you,
B♭           E♭/G           A♭    B♭/A♭    A♭    B♭/A♭
I will never leave you alone.
```

Verse 2

```
C
Sometimes I just forget,
G
Say things I might regret,
C                      F          C/G  G
It breaks my heart__ to see you cry - ing.
C               F/A
I don't want to lose you,
B♭            E♭/G            A♭    B♭/A♭    A♭    B♭/A♭
I could never make it alone.
```

Chorus 1

```
C
I am a man

F                    C               G
   Who would fight     for your hon  -  or,

C             F            Dm7              G7
I'll be the he - ro you're__ dreaming of.

Am7            Dm7
We'll live forev - er,

C              E/G♯
Knowing togeth - er,

       Am7          Dm7
That we     did it all

            G7           C         F/A  B♭
For thc glo - ry of love.
```

Verse 3

```
C
     You keep me standing tall,

G
     You help me through it all,

C                      F
     I'm always strong

                  C/G   G
When you're be-side    me.

C                  F/A
     I have always needed you,

B♭                E♭/G         A♭     B♭/A♭     A♭     B♭/A♭
     I could never make it alone.
```

Chorus 2

```
C
I am a man

F                    C               G
   Who would fight     for your hon  -  or,

C             F            Dm7              G7
I'll be the he - ro you're__ dreaming of.
```

Am7 Dm7
We'll live forev - er,

C E/G♯
Knowing togeth - er,

Am7 Dm7
That we did it all

G7 C F C
For the glo - ry of love.

Bridge

Fm Ab
Just like a knight in shining armor,

Bb Eb
From a long time a-go,

Fm Ab
Just in time I will save the day,

Cm7 Fm7 Bb Eb
Take you to my castle far away.

| Bb F7sus4 F7 | Bb Eb/G | C Ab |

Chorus 3

Db
I am the man

Gb Db Ab7
Who will fight for your hon - or,

Db Bbm Ebm7 Ab7
I'll be the he - ro that you're__ dreaming of.

```
          B♭m7           E♭m7
We're gonna live forev - er,

D♭               F/A
Knowing togeth - er,

            B♭m7            E♭m7
That we            did it all

            A♭7sus4   A♭7    D♭    G♭
For the glo  -  ry     of love.
```

Interlude | D♭ A♭7sus4 A♭7 | D♭ B♭m7 | E♭m7 A♭7sus4 A♭7 |

Outro

```
B♭m7             E♭m7
We'll live forev - er,

D♭               F/A
Knowing togeth - er,

           B♭m7       E♭m7
That we      did it all

               A♭7sus4  A♭7     B♭m7
For the glo  -  ry          of love.

        G♭   A♭            B♭m7
||: We did it all for love.              :||    Repeat and fade
```

Have I Told You Lately

Words and Music by
Van Morrison

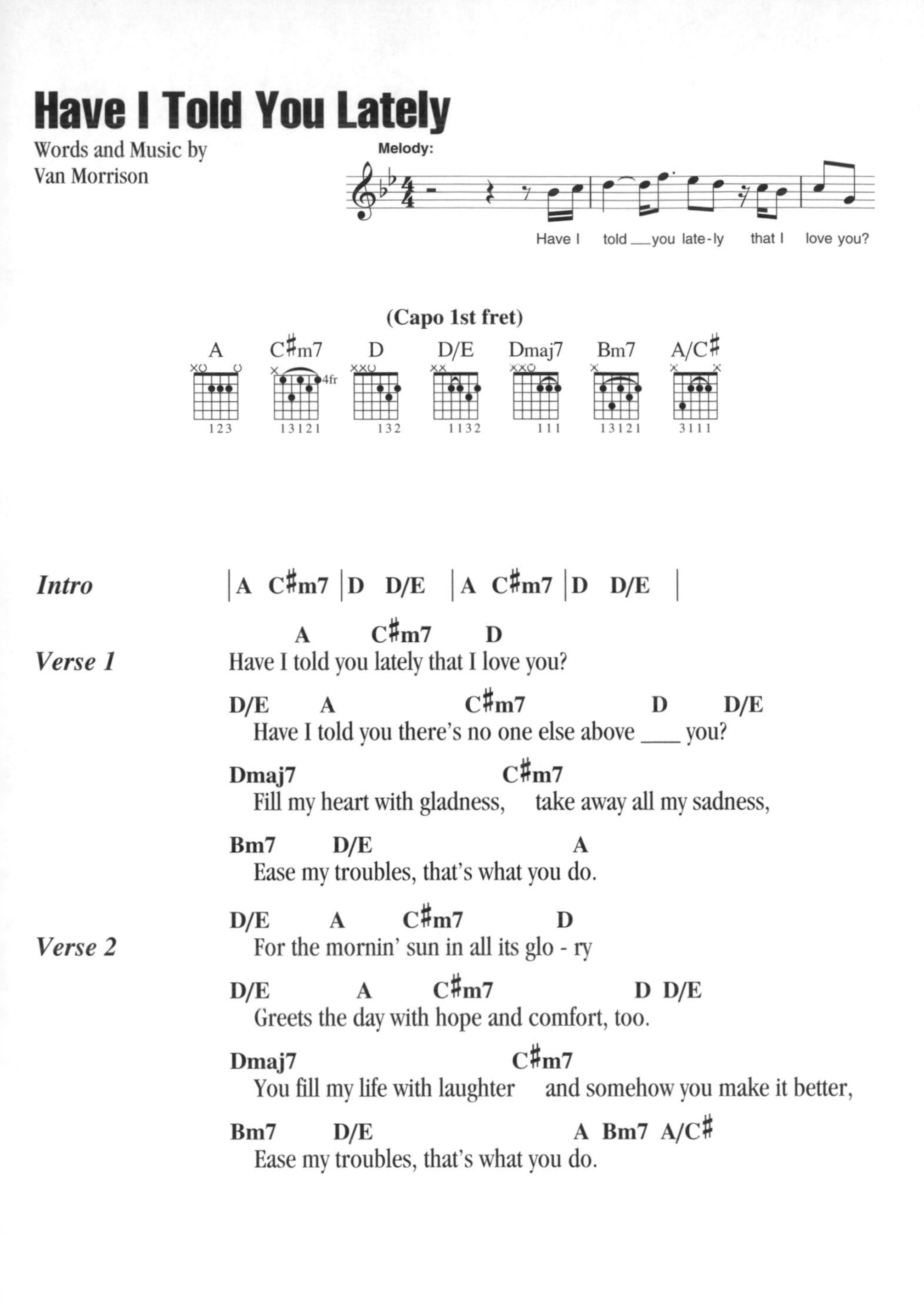

Intro |**A C#m7** |**D D/E** |**A C#m7** |**D D/E** |

Verse 1

A C#m7 D
Have I told you lately that I love you?

D/E A C#m7 D D/E
Have I told you there's no one else above ___ you?

Dmaj7 C#m7
Fill my heart with gladness, take away all my sadness,

Bm7 D/E A
Ease my troubles, that's what you do.

Verse 2

D/E A C#m7 D
For the mornin' sun in all its glo - ry

D/E A C#m7 D D/E
Greets the day with hope and comfort, too.

Dmaj7 C#m7
You fill my life with laughter and somehow you make it better,

Bm7 D/E A Bm7 A/C#
Ease my troubles, that's what you do.

Bridge 1

```
Dmaj7
  There's a love that's divine
                                    C#m7             Bm7  C#m7
And it's yours and it's mine ___ like the sun.
Dmaj7
  And at the end of the day we should give thanks and pray
C#m7      D/E
To the one, to the one.
```

Verse 3 *Repeat Verse 1*

Guitar Solo *Repeat Verse 2 (Instrumental)*

Bridge 2 *Repeat Bridge 1 (Instrumental)*

Verse 4

```
              A       C#m7     D
And have I told you lately that I love you?
D/E     A               C#m7         D        D/E
  Have I told you there's no one else a - bove you?
Dmaj7                         C#m7
  You fill my heart with gladness,   take away my sadness,
Bm7      D/E                          A  Bm7  A/C#
  Ease my troubles, that's what you do.
Dmaj7                     C#m7
  Take away all my sadness,   fill my life with gladness,
Bm7      D/E                          A  Bm7  A/C#
  Ease my troubles that's what you do.
Dmaj7                     C#m7
  Take away all my sadness,   fill my life with gladness,
Bm7      D/E                          A
  Ease my troubles that's what you do.
```

Heart and Soul

from the Paramount Short Subject A SONG IS BORN

Words by Frank Loesser
Music by Hoagy Carmichael

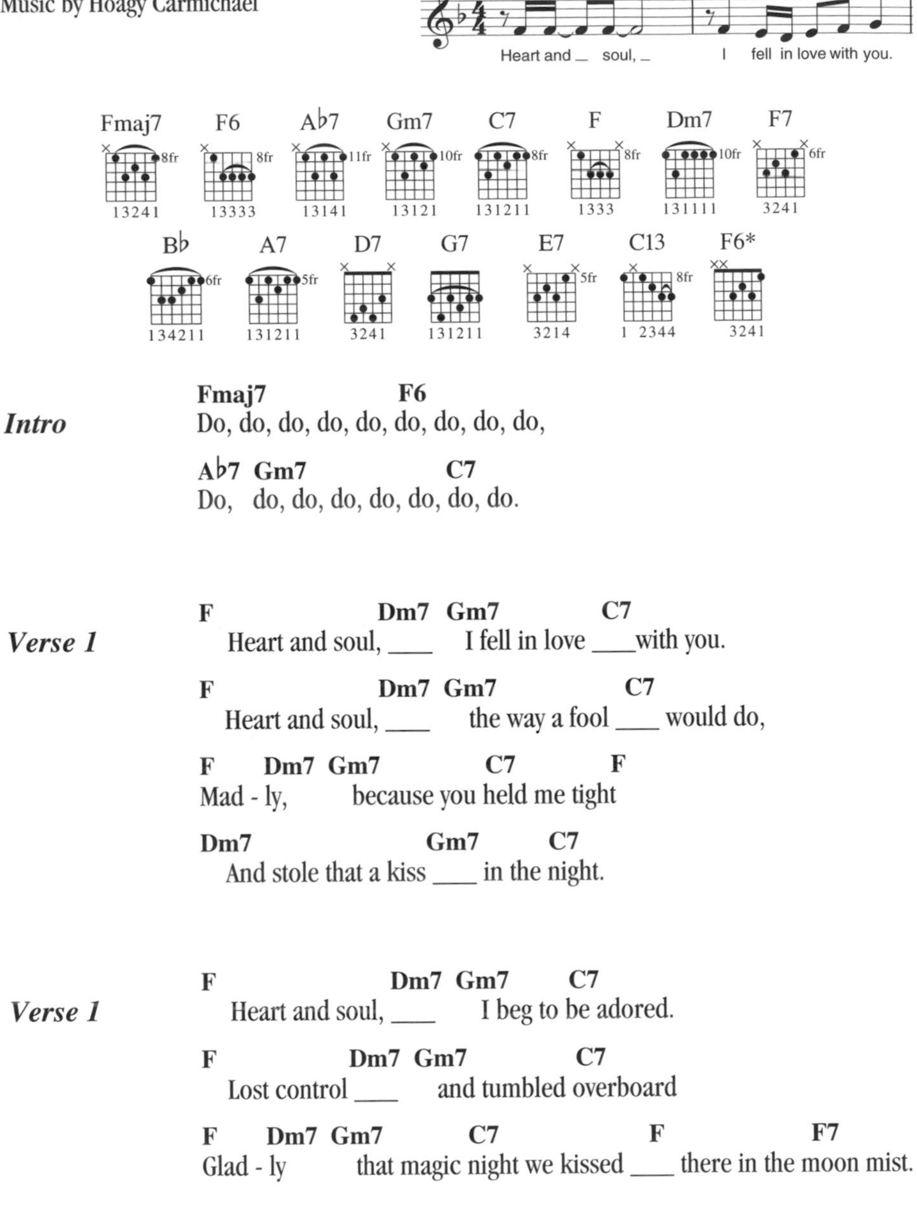

Intro

Fmaj7 **F6**
Do, do, do, do, do, do, do, do, do,

A♭7 **Gm7** **C7**
Do, do, do, do, do, do, do, do.

Verse 1

F **Dm7** **Gm7** **C7**
Heart and soul, ___ I fell in love ___with you.

F **Dm7** **Gm7** **C7**
Heart and soul, ___ the way a fool ___ would do,

F **Dm7** **Gm7** **C7** **F**
Mad - ly, because you held me tight

Dm7 **Gm7** **C7**
And stole that a kiss ___ in the night.

Verse 1

F **Dm7** **Gm7** **C7**
Heart and soul, ___ I beg to be adored.

F **Dm7** **Gm7** **C7**
Lost control ___ and tumbled overboard

F **Dm7** **Gm7** **C7** **F** **F7**
Glad - ly that magic night we kissed ___ there in the moon mist.

Bridge

```
Bb                A7        D7    G7
   Oh, but your lips were thrill - ing,

C7              F7  E7      A7
   How much too  thrill - ing.

Bb              A7        D7    G7
   Never be - fore were mine so

C7          F7  E7   C7
   Strange - ly   will - ing.
```

Verse 3

```
F                   Dm7  Gm7                     C7
   But now I see ___       what one embrace ___ can do.

F                Dm7  Gm7          C7        F     Dm7
   Look at me, ___      it's got me loving you mad - ly.

Gm7         C7           A7
   That little kiss you stole

Gm7        C7          F    Dm7  Gm7  C7
   Held all my heart and soul.
```

Verse 4

```
F                Dm7  Gm7     C7
Heart and soul, ___     I fell in love with you.

F               Dm7  Gm7          C7
Heart and soul, ___      the way a fool would do,

F         Dm7  Gm7            C7          F
   Mad - ly,       because you held me tight

Dm7                        C7
   And stole that a kiss ___ in the night.
```

Verse 5

```
F                Dm7  Gm7       C7
Heart and soul, ___      I beg to be adored.

F            Dm7  Gm7          C7
Lost control ___      and tumbled overboard

F         Dm7  Gm7       C7       A7
   Glad - ly         that little kiss you stole

Gm7                    C13     F    F6*
   Held all my heart ___ and soul.
```

Here, There and Everywhere

Words and Music by
John Lennon and
Paul McCartney

Melody:

To lead a bet-ter life, _ I need my love to be here. ___

G Bm B♭ Am7 D7 Am C

21 3 | 13421 | 12341 | 2314 | 213 | 231 | 32 1

F♯m7 B7 Em F7 Gm Cm

131111 | 213 4 | 23 | 131211 | 134111 | 13421

Intro

```
G          Bm
  To lead a better life,
B♭                         Am7  D7
  I need my love to be here.
```

Verse 1

```
G     Am
Here,
Bm                C              G   Am
Making each day__ of the year.
Bm                C                 F♯m7        B7
Changing my life__ with a wave__ of her hand.
F♯m7        B7        Em                    Am             Am7  D7
Nobody can__ deny__ that there's some - thing there.
```

Verse 2

```
G     Am
There,
Bm                  C                   G    Am
Running my hands__ through her hair.
Bm                 C                F♯m7       B7
Both of us think - ing how good__ it can be.
F♯m7                  B7        Em                 Am              Am7  D7
Someone is speak-ing, but she doesn't know__ he's there.
```

Bridge 1

F7 B♭ Gm
I want her ev'rywhere,

Cm D7 Gm
And if she's beside me, I know I need never care.

Cm D7
But to love her is to need her

Verse 3

G Am
Ev'rywhere.

Bm C G Am
Knowing that love__ is to share.

Bm C F♯m7 B7
Each one believ - ing that love__ never dies,

F♯m7 B7 Em Am Am7 D7
Watching their eyes__ and hoping I'm al - ways there.

Bridge 2

F7 B♭ Gm
I want her ev'rywhere,

Cm D7 Gm
And if she's beside me, I know I need never care.

Cm D7
But to love her is to need her

Verse 4

G Am
Ev'rywhere.

Bm C G Am
Knowing that love__ is to share.

Bm C F♯m7 B7
Each one believ - ing that love__ never dies.

F♯m7 B7 Em Am Am7 D7
Watching her eyes__ and hoping I'm al - ways there.

G Am
I will be there

Bm C
And ev'rywhere.

G Am Bm C G
Here, there and ev'rywhere.

Hopelessly Devoted to You

from GREASE

Words and Music by John Farrar

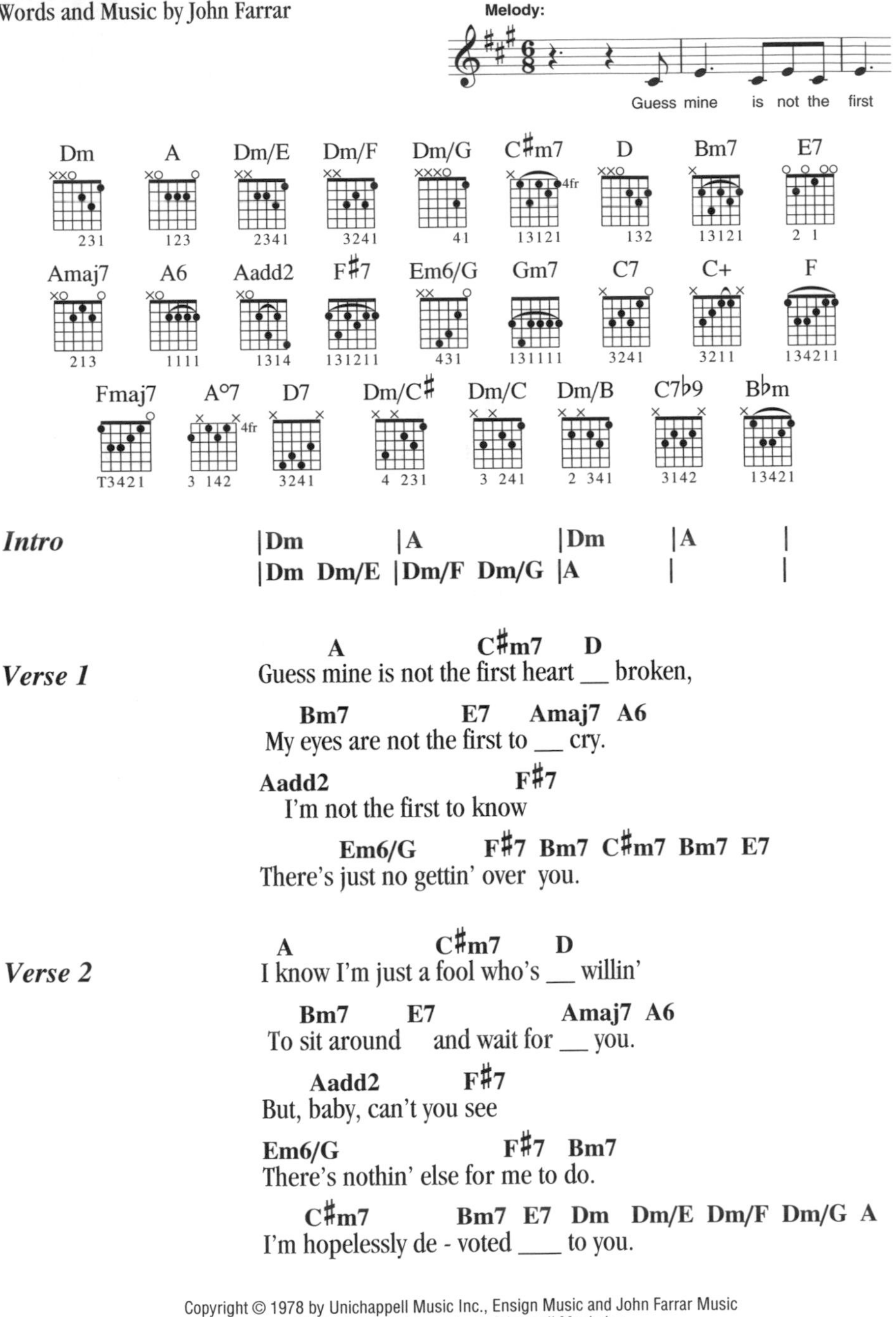

Intro

```
|Dm          |A              |Dm       |A        |
|Dm  Dm/E    |Dm/F  Dm/G     |A        |         |
```

Verse 1

```
             A               C♯m7      D
Guess mine is not the first heart __ broken,
   Bm7              E7     Amaj7  A6
My eyes are not the first to __ cry.
Aadd2                    F♯7
  I'm not the first to know
           Em6/G          F♯7  Bm7  C♯m7  Bm7  E7
There's just no gettin' over  you.
```

Verse 2

```
 A              C♯m7       D
I know I'm just a fool who's __ willin'
  Bm7        E7               Amaj7  A6
To sit around    and wait for __ you.
   Aadd2           F♯7
But, baby, can't you see
Em6/G                 F♯7   Bm7
There's nothin' else for me to do.
    C♯m7            Bm7  E7   Dm   Dm/E  Dm/F  Dm/G  A
I'm hopelessly de - voted ___ to you.
```

Chorus 1

```
N.C.                Gm7
But now there's nowhere to hide

                                    C7  C+
Since you pushed my love aside.

     F              Fmaj7
I'm __ out of my head,

A°7                D7   Gm7
Hopelessly de - voted to you,

                   C7   Dm  Dm/C#  Dm/C  Dm/B
Hopelessly de - voted to you.

Gm7                C7   Dm   Dm/E  Dm/F  Dm/G  A
Hopelessly de - voted to you.
```

Verse 3

```
    A              C#m7    D
My head is sayin',   "Fool, ___ forget him."

    Bm7             E7            Amaj7  A6
My heart is sayin',   "Don't let go.

Aadd2          F#7
Hold on to the end."

Em6/G              F#7      Bm7
   That's what I in - tend to do.

C#m7               Bm7  E7  Dm   Dm/E  Dm/F  Dm/G  A
Hopelessly de - voted ___ to you.
```

Chorus 2

```
N.C.                Gm7
But now there's nowhere to hide

                                    C7  C+
Since you pushed my love aside.

     F              Fmaj7
I'm __ out of my head,

A°7                D7      Gm7
Hopelessly de - voted to __ you,

                   C7b9   Dm  Dm/C#  Dm/C  Dm/B
Hopelessly de - voted to you.

Gm7                C7b9  Bbm   F
Hopelessly de - voted         to you.
```

How Deep Is Your Love

from the Motion Picture SATURDAY NIGHT FEVER

Words and Music by Barry Gibb,
Robin Gibb and Maurice Gibb

Melody:

I know your eyes in the morn - ing sun.

(Capo 1st fret)

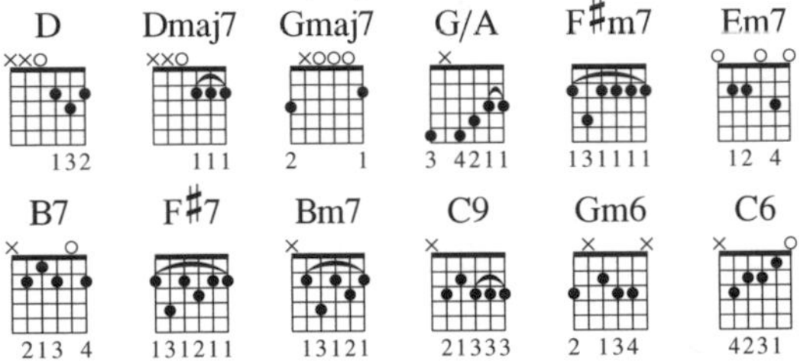

D 132 | Dmaj7 111 | Gmaj7 2 1 | G/A 3 4211 | F#m7 131111 | Em7 12 4

B7 213 4 | F#7 131211 | Bm7 13121 | C9 21333 | Gm6 2 134 | C6 4231

Intro

||: D | Dmaj7 | Gmaj7 | G/A :||

Verse 1

```
                 D          F#m7       Em7
I know your eyes in the morning sun.
B7              Em7              F#7          G/A
I feel you touch ___ me in the pouring rain.
               D                F#m7       Bm7
And the mo - ment that you wander far ___ from me,
            Em7                   G/A
I wanna feel you in my arms again.
```

Pre-Chorus 1

```
                 Gmaj7                    F#m7
And you come ___ to me on a sum - mer breeze,

                   Em7                               C9
Keep me warm ___ in your love, then you soft - ly leave.

          F#m7                    G/A
And it's me you need to show.     (How deep is your love?)
```

Chorus 1

```
               D
How deep ___ is your love?

             Dmaj7
How deep ___ is your love?

Gmaj7                  Gm6
I really mean to learn.

                D                        C6
'Cause we're living in a world of fools,

              B7                                     Em7
Breaking us down when they all should let us be.

             Gm6
We belong ___ to you and me.
```

Verse 2

```
D          F#m7     Em7
   I be - lieve in you.

B7                   Em7          F#7    G/A
You know the door ___ to my ver - y soul.

                    D                F#m7     Bm7
You're the light ___ in my deep - est, dark - est hour,

                Em7           G/A
You're my sav - ior when I fall.
```

Pre-Chorus 2

```
                Gmaj7                F♯m7
And you may ___ not think I care ___ for you

                   Em7                    C9
When you know ___ down inside that I real - ly do.

              F♯m7                G/A
And it's me ___ you need to show.    (How deep is your love?)
```

Chorus 2

Repeat Chorus 1

Verse 3

Repeat Verse 1 w/vocal ad lib.

Pre-Chorus 3

Repeat Pre-Chorus 1

Outro-Chorus

```
                D
‖: How deep ___ is your love?

            Dmaj7
How deep ___ is your love?

Gmaj7               Gm6
I really mean to learn.

            D                       C6
'Cause we're living in a world of fools,

            B7                               Em7
Breaking us down when they all should let us be.

            Gm6              D  F♯m7  G/A
We belong ___ to you and me.              :‖ Repeat and fade
```

I Do (Cherish You)

Words and Music by
Robert Stegall and Dan Hill

Intro

Gadd2
I do, I do.

Em7 **Am7add4** **Cm/E♭** **Dm** **C**
I do, I do. ____ Mm.

Verse 1

G **Am7**
All I am, ____ all I'll be,

Bm7 **C/D**
Ev'ry - thing in this world, all that I'll ever need

G **Am7**
Is in your eyes shining at me.

Bm7 **C/D**
When you smile I can feel all my passion unfolding.

C **Gadd2/B**
Your hand brushes mine,

C **Dsus2**
And a thousand sensations se - duce me 'cause I…

Chorus 1

```
       G               Em7
I do ___ cherish you.

         Am7                       C/D
For the rest of my life you don't have to think twice.

         G                Em7          Am7
I will ___ love you still, ___ from the depths of my soul.

         B7sus4         B7
It's be - yond my con - trol.

                Em           Bm/D        C#m7b5
I've waited so ___ long to say this to you.

          Am7                                   D          Gadd2
If you're asking do I love you this much, ___ I do.

Em7        Am7add4   Bb  Dm  C/E
   Oh, baby. ___ Oh.
```

Verse 2

```
                 G            Am7
In my world ___ before you,

              Bm7
I lived out - side my emotions.

               C/D
Didn't know where I was going

          G              Am7
'Till that day I found you.

             Bm7              C/D
How you opened my life to a new paradise.

C                          Gadd2/B
   In a world torn by change,

            C               Dsus2
Still with all my heart until my dying day,
```

Chorus 2

G Em7
I do ___ cherish you.

Am7 C/D
For the rest of my life you don't have to think twice.

G Em7 Am7
I will ___ love you still, ___ from the depths of my soul.

B7sus4 B7
It's be - yond my con - trol.

Em Bm/D C♯m7♭5
I've waited so ___ long to say this to you.

Am7 D7sus4
If you're asking do I love you this much, ___ I do.

B♭maj7 B♭7
Yes, I do. (I real - ly love you.)

Am7 A♭7♯5
I do. ___ (I real - ly love you.)

Gm7 D7sus4 E7sus4
If you're asking do I love you this much, _____ baby,

Outro-Chorus

A F♯m7
I do ___ cherish you.

Bm7 C♯7sus4 C♯7
From the depths of my soul, it's be - yond my con - trol.

F♯m F♯m/E D♯m7♭5
I've waited so ___ long to say this to you.

Bm7 E7sus4
If you're asking do I love you this much,

A F♯m7 D E7sus4 E7 A
Baby, I do. _______ Ah, __________ I do.

I Don't Know Why (I Just Do)

Lyric by Roy Turk
Music by Fred E. Ahlert

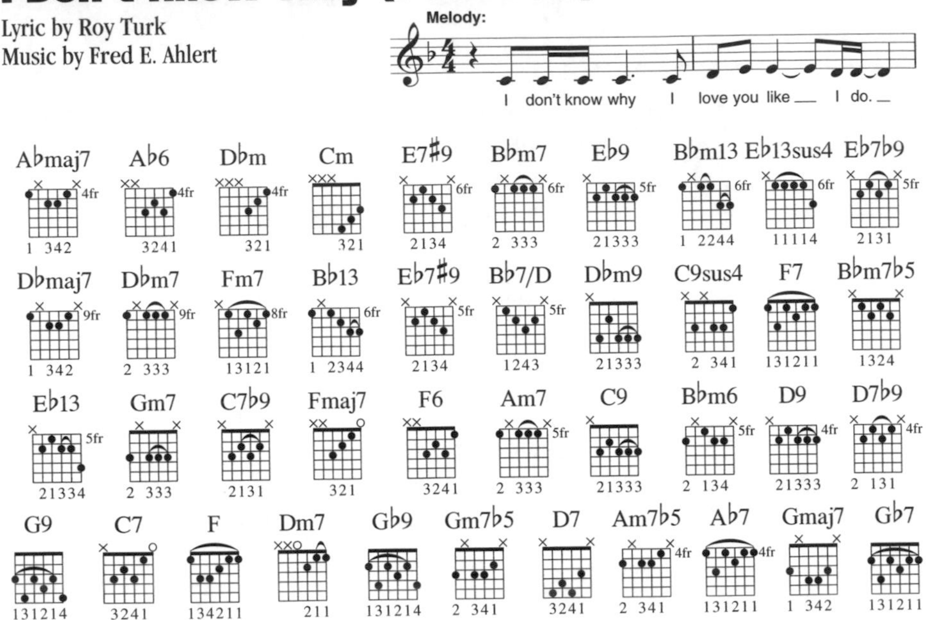

Intro

Abmaj7	Ab6 Dbm	Cm E7#9	Bbm7 Eb9
Bbm13	Eb13sus4	Bbm7 Eb7b9	Abmaj7
Dbmaj7 Dbm7 Fm7	Bb13 Eb7#9	Abmaj7 Fm7	Bb7/D Eb9 Eb7b9
Abmaj7 Dbm9	C9sus4 F7	Bbm7b5 Eb13	Abmaj7 Gm7 C7b9

Chorus 1

Fmaj7 **F6**
I don't know why I love you like I do.

Am7 **Abm6** **Gm7**
I don't know why, ___ I just do.

I don't know why you thrill me like you do.

C9 **C7b9** **F6**
I don't know why ___ you just do.

Verse 1

```
      B♭m6       D9     D7♭9  G9          C7
You ne - ver seem to want my _____ romancing,

F                Dm7        Gm7             G9    G♭9
   The only time you hold me    is when we're danc - ing.
```

Chorus 2

```
Fmaj7             Am7                D9  D7♭9
I don't know why    I love you like I do.

Gm7♭5  C7♭9               C7      F      D7  Gm7  C7♭9
          I don't know why, I just ___ do.
```

Guitar Solo 1

Repeat Chorus 1 (Instrumental)

Piano Solo

Repeat Verse 1 (Instrumental)

Guitar Solo 2

```
|Fmaj7                  |Am7♭5     D7♭9  D7   |
|Gm7♭5      C7          |F   A♭7   Gmaj7  G♭7 |
```

Verse 2

```
F6     B♭m6        D9      D7♭9  G9          C7
   You ne - ver seem to want my _____ romancing,

F               Dm7         Gm7            G9    G♭9
   The only time you hold me    is when we're danc - ing.
```

Chorus 3

```
Fmaj7              Am7               D9      D7♭9
I don't know why    I love you like __ I do.

Gm7♭5            C7♭9  C7    Fmaj7
      I don't know why, I  just do.
```

I Honestly Love You

Words and Music by Jeff Barry and Peter Allen

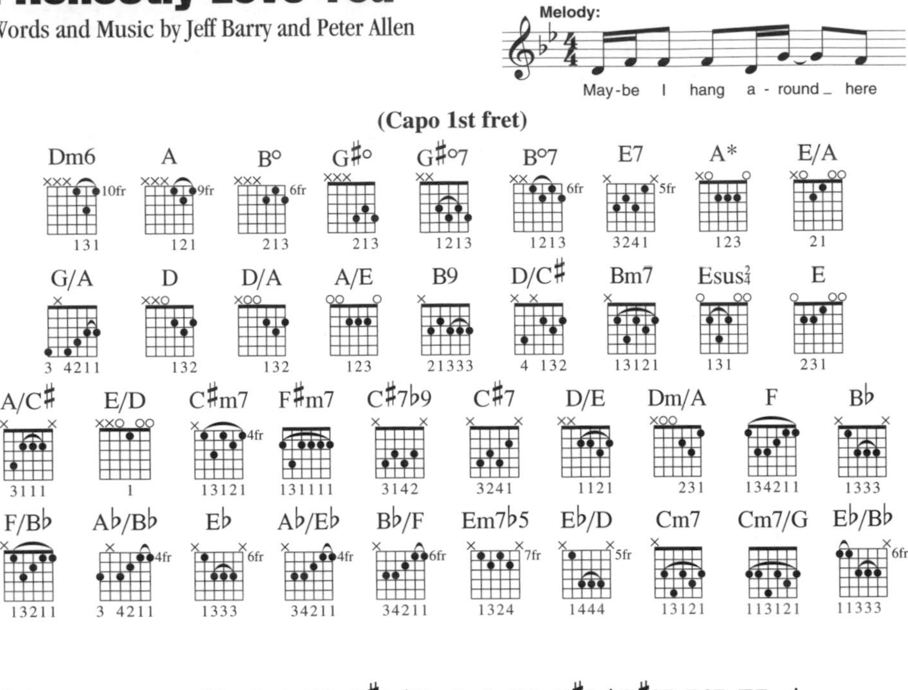

Intro

|Dm6 A B° G♯° |Dm6 A B° G♯° |G♯°7 B°7 E7 |

Verse 1

A* E/A
Maybe I hang around here a little more than I should.

G/A D G/A D/A
We both know I got somewhere else __ to go.

A/E B9
But I got somethin' to tell you that I never thought I would,

D D/C♯ Bm7 A* Esus4/2 E
But I believe you really ought to know.

Chorus 1

A* E/A D/A A* E/A D/A
I love you, I honestly love ___ you.

Verse 2

A* E/A
You don't have to answer; I see it in your eyes.

G/A D
Maybe it was better left un - said.

A/E B9
But this is pure and simple and you must realize

D D/C#
That it's comin' from my heart

Bm7 A/C# A/E Esus$^{2}_{4}$ E
And not my ___ head.

Chorus 2

A* E/A D/A A* E/A G/A A*
I love you, I honestly love ___ you.

Bridge

D E/D C#m7
I'm not tryin' to make you feel un - comf'rtable.

F#m7 D E A*
I'm not tryin' to make you an - ything at all.

C#7b9 C#7 F#m7 A/E E/D D
But this feel - in' doesn't come ___ along ev'ry day,

A/C#
And you shouldn't blow the chance

Bm7 D/E
When you've got the chance to say,

Chorus 3

A* E/A
(Ooh, I love you. Ooh, I love you.)

D/A Dm/A A* F
(Ooh, I love you, I honestly do.) I honestly love ___ you.

Verse 3

```
Bb                                 F/Bb
   If we both were born in an - other place and time,
     Ab/Bb                      Eb            Ab/Eb   Eb
This moment might be ending     in a kiss.
     Bb/F                     Em7b5
But there you are with yours,    here I am with mine,
     Eb                  Eb/D       Cm7       Bb     Cm7/G    F
So I guess we'll just be leaving it at ___ this.
```

Outro-Chorus

```
Bb             F/Bb  Eb/Bb              Bb
   I love you,          I honestly love ___ you.
F/Bb  Eb/Bb              Bb      F/Bb  Eb/Bb          Bb
          I honestly love __ you.              I honestly    love you.
```

I Won't Last a Day Without You

Words and Music by Paul Williams
and Roger Nichols

Intro ‖: D F#m7 D/F# | G G/A A :‖

Verse 1

D F#m7 G A
Day after day ___ I must face a world of stran - gers

Bm9 Em7 G/A A
Where I don't belong; I'm not that strong.

D F#m7 G A
It's nice to know ___ that there's someone I can turn ___ to

Bm9 Em7
Who will always care; you're always there.

Chorus 1

G/A A D C/D G
When there's no getting o - ver that rainbow,

Em7 A D C/D G
When my smallest of dreams ___ won't come ___ true,

Em7 G/A D C/D Gmaj7 D/F#
I can take all the mad - ness the world has to give,

Em7 G/A D F#m7 D/F# G G/A A
But I won't last a day without you.

| D F#m7 D/F# | G G/A A |

Verse 2

```
D                  F#m7          G             A
   So many times ___ when the city seems to be __ without
  Bm9           Em7          G/A  A
A friendly face, a lonely place,
D                  F#m7          G               A
   It's nice to know ___ that you'll be there if I need __ you,
           Bm9                 Em7
And you'll always smile, it's all worthwhile.
```

Chorus 2

```
G/A  A          D            C/D      G
      When there's no getting o - ver that rainbow,
Em7  A       D                  C/D                G
      When my smallest of dreams ___ won't come ___ true,
Em7  G/A  D                  C/D        Gmaj7          D/F#
      I can  take all the mad - ness the world has to give,
     Em7    G/A         D
But I won't last a day without you.
```

Bridge

```
Bm7add4  D/E  E/G#  A     C#m7
Touch me   and I end up singing.
Bm7              E7                F#7sus4  F#7
Troubles seem to up and disappear.
     G#m7   C#7                  F#
You touch me with the love you're bringing.
D#m7         E                 F#7sus4
I can't really lose when you're near.
F#7                Em7  A7  D
    (When you're near   my  love.)
```

Verse 3

F♯m7 G A
If all my friends ___ have forgot - ten half their prom - ises,

Bm9 Em7 G/A A
They're not ___ unkind, just hard to find.

D F♯m7 G A
One look at you ___ and I know that I could learn to live

Bm9 Em7
Without ___ the rest, I found the best.

Chorus 3

G/A A D C/D G
When there's no getting o - ver that rainbow,

Em7 A D C/D G
When my smallest of dreams ___ won't come ___ true,

Em7 G/A D C/D Gmaj7 D/F♯
I can take all the mad - ness the world has to give,

Em7 G/A
But I won't last a day without you.

Chorus 4

D C/D G
When there's no getting o - ver that rainbow,

Em7 A D C/D G
When my smallest of dreams ___ won't come ___ true,

Em7 G/A D C/D Gmaj7 D/F♯
I can take all the mad - ness the world has to give,

Em7 G/A D F♯m7 D/F♯
But I won't last a day without you.

G G/A D
(Won't last a day without you.

F♯m7 D/F♯ G G/A A D
With - out you.)

I Love How You Love Me

Words and Music by Barry Mann and Larry Kolber

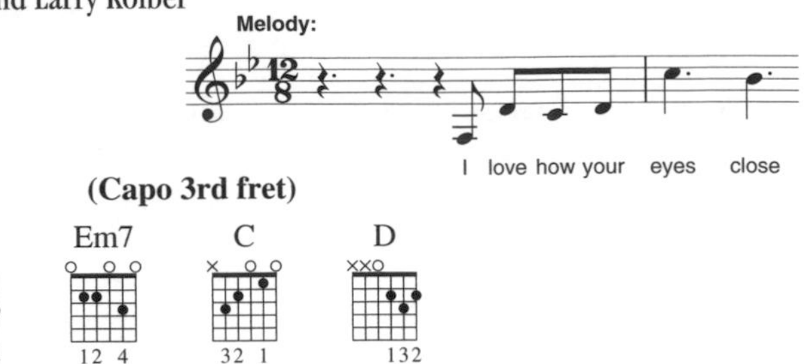


```
           N.C.               G                           Em7
Verse 1    I love how your eyes close whenever you kiss me.

                              C                              D
           And when I'm a - way from you, I love how you ___ miss me.

                         G                       Em7
           I love the way you always treat me tenderly.

                         C           D                  G
           But, darling, most of all,   I love how you love me. (I love how you love me.)


           N.C.                G                           Em7
Verse 2       I love how your heart beats whenever I hold you.

                            C                         D
           I love how you think of me without being told to.

                         G                        Em7
           I love the way your touch is always heavenly.

                         C           D                  G
           But, darling, most of all,   I love how you love me.

                                     N.C.
           (I love how you love me.)
```

```
             G                                   Em7
*Verse 3*      I love how your eyes close    whenever you kiss me.

             C                                        D
               And when I'm away from you, I love how you miss me.

                       G                                  Em7
             I love the way your touch is always heavenly.

                          C          D
             But, darling, most of all,


                           G
*Outro-Verse* I love how you love me. (I love how you love me.)

                      Em7
             I love how you hug me. (I love how you hug me.)

                           C                                        D
             I love how you squeeze me, tease me, please me, love __ how you love me.

                      G
             I love how you love me.    Fade out
```

I'll Be There

Words and Music by Berry Gordy,
Hal Davis, Willie Hutch and Bob West

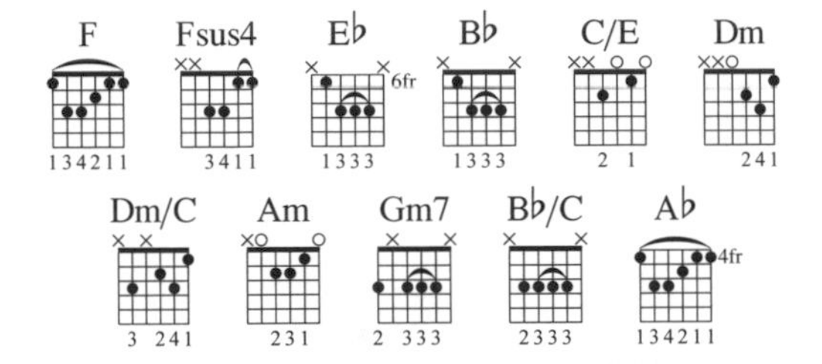

Intro | F Fsus4 F | E♭ B♭ | F Fsus4 F | Fsus4 |

Verse 1

```
F                C/E
  You and I must make a pact.
Dm        Dm/C     Am          B♭
  We must bring sal - vation back.
Gm7            B♭/C     F
Where there is love, I'll ___ be there. (I'll be there.)
```

Verse 2

```
F                 C/E
  I'll reach out my hand to you,
Dm          Dm/C  Am        B♭
  I'll have faith in all you do.
Gm7            B♭/C           F
  Just call my name and I'll ___ be there. (I'll be there.)
```

Bridge 1

```
         A♭              E♭
And oh,  I'll be there to comfort you,

          B♭
Build my world of dreams around you.

     F
I'm so glad that I found you.

A♭                  E♭
   I'll be there with a love that's strong.

            B♭                  F           Fsus4
I'll be your strength, I'll keep holdin' on.

                                                         F
(Holdin' on, holdin' on, holdin' on.) Yes, I will. Yes, ___ I will.
```

Verse 3

```
F                         C/E
   Let me fill your heart ___ with joy and laughter.

Dm           Dm/C    Am                     B♭
   Together - ness,      well it's all I'm after.

        Gm7     B♭/C         F
When - ever you need me I'll ___ be there. (I'll be there.)
```

Verse 4

```
F                            C/E
   I'll be there to protect ___ you.

Dm          Dm/C          Am                  B♭
   With an un - selfish love ___ that respects you.

Gm7          B♭/C      F
   Just call my name and I'll be there. (I'll be there.)
```

Bridge 2

```
         A♭              E♭
And oh,  I'll be there to comfort you,

          B♭
Build my world of dreams around you.

     F
I'm so glad that I found you.

A♭                  E♭
   I'll be there with a love that's strong.

      B♭                        F        Fsus4
I'll be your strength, I'll keep holdin' on. Ooh.

                                   F
(Holdin' on, holdin' on,) Yes, I will.
```

Verse 5

```
F                       C/E
  If you should ever find someone new,
Dm            Dm/C    Am          B♭
  I know he better be good to you,
Gm7            B♭/C               F
  'Cause if he ___ doesn't, I'll ___ be there. (I'll be there.)
```

Don't you know baby, yeah, yeah.

Outro

```
F               C/E  Dm   Dm/C     Am  B♭
  I'll be there, _____    I'll be there.
Gm7             B♭/C            F
  Just call my name, I'll be there.
```

Just look over your shoulders, honey.

```
                     C/E  Dm   Dm/C     Am  B♭
Ooh, I'll be there, _____    I'll be there.
         Gm7    B♭/C          F
When - ever you need me I'll ___ be there.
```

Don't you know baby, yeah, yeah.

```
F               C/E  Dm   Dm/C     Am  B♭
  I'll be there, _____    I'll be there.
Gm7             B♭/C       F
  Just call my name, I'll ___ be there.
              C/E  Dm   Dm/C     Am  B♭
I'll be there, _____    I'll be there.       Fade out
```

Just Once

Words by Cynthia Weil
Music by Barry Mann

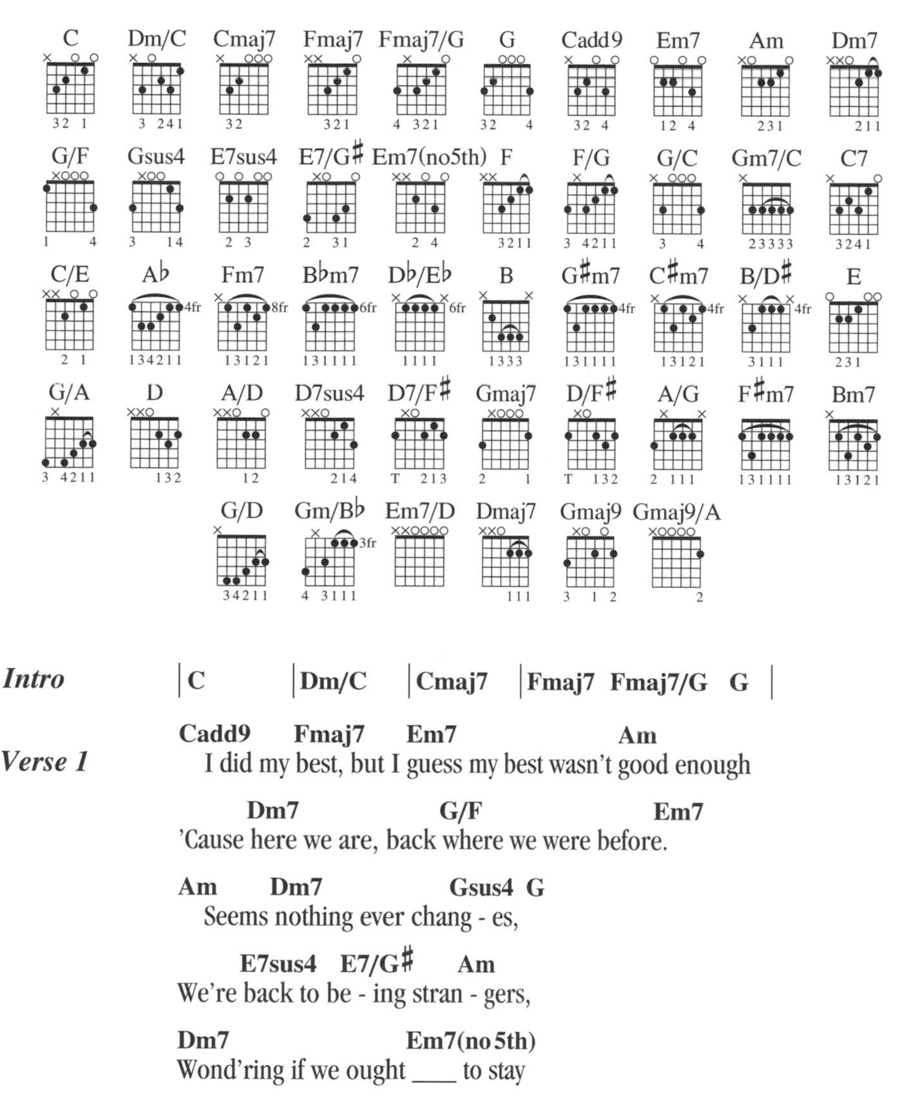

Intro | C | Dm/C | Cmaj7 | Fmaj7 Fmaj7/G G |

Verse 1

Cadd9 Fmaj7 Em7 Am
I did my best, but I guess my best wasn't good enough

Dm7 G/F Em7
'Cause here we are, back where we were before.

Am Dm7 Gsus4 G
Seems nothing ever chang - es,

E7sus4 E7/G♯ Am
We're back to be - ing stran - gers,

Dm7 Em7(no 5th)
Wond'ring if we ought ____ to stay

F F/G G F/G G
Or head on out the door.

Chorus 1

C G/C Gm7/C C7 Fmaj7
Just once can we figure out what we ___ keep doin' wrong?

C/E Dm7 G/F Em7
Why we never last ___ for very long.

Am Dm7 F/G
What are we do - in' wrong?

C G/C Gm7/C C7 Fmaj7
Just once can't we find a way to fi - n'lly make it right?

C/E Dm7 G/F Em7 Am
Make the magic last ___ for more than just one night.

Dm7 F/G
If we could just get to it, I know we could break through it.

| C | Dm/C | Cmaj7 | Fmaj7 Fmaj7/G G |

Verse 2

Cadd9 Fmaj7 Em7 Am
I gave my all, but I think my all may have been ___ too much

Dm7 G/F Em7
'Cause Lord knows we're not getting anywhere.

Am Dm7 Gsus4 G
It seems we're always blow - in'

E7sus4 E7/G♯ Am
What - ever we've ___ got go - in',

Dm7 Em7(no5th)
And it seems at times with all ___ we've got

F F/G G F/G G
We haven't got a prayer.

Chorus 2

C G/C Gm7/C C7 Fmaj7
Just once can we figure out what we ___ keep doin' wrong?

C/E Dm7 G/F Em7
Why the good times nev - er last for long.

Am Dm7 F/G G
Where are we go - in' wrong?

C G/C Gm7/C C7 Fmaj7
Just once can't we find a way to fi - n'lly make it right?

C/E Dm7 G/F Em7 Am
To make the magic last ___ for more than just one night.

Dm7 F/G
I know we could break through it if we could just get to it.

Bridge

```
    A♭              Fm7
Just once I want to understand

B♭m7      D♭/E♭              A♭
Why it always comes back to good - bye.

B                        G♯m7
Why can't we get our - selves in hand

C♯m7      B/D♯
And admit to one another

E                        B/D♯
We're no good without ___ each other?

C♯m7                        B/D♯
   Take the best and make ___ it better,

Em7              G/A
Find a way to stay ___ together.
```

Chorus 3

```
D      A/D         D7sus4        D7/F♯        Gmaj7
   Just once can we find a way to fi - n'lly make it right?

   D/F♯  Em7                   A/G                F♯m7      Bm7
Oh,      to make the magic last ___ for more than just one night.

  Em7
I know we could break through it

  G/A                          D  A/D  G/D  A/D
If we could just get to it just once.

D        A/D        Gm/B♭ G/A
   Whoa, ___ we can get to  it

    D      Em7/D  Dmaj7  Gmaj9  Gmaj9/A  G/A  B
Just once.
```

I'm Still in Love with You

Words and Music by Al Green,
Willie Mitchell and Al Jackson, Jr.

Melody:

Spend - ing my day

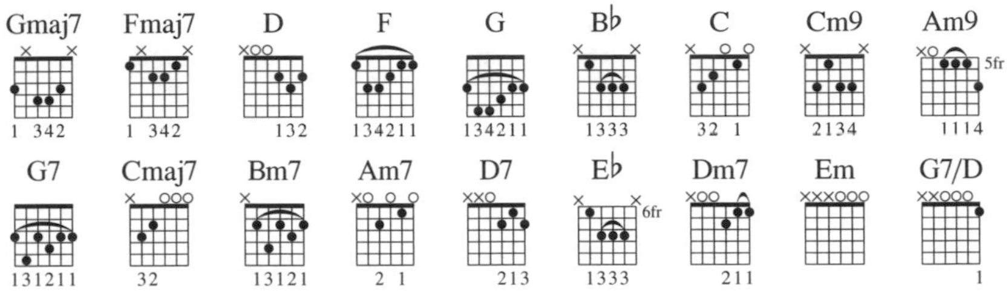

Gmaj7 Fmaj7 D F G B♭ C Cm9 Am9

1 342 | 1 342 | 132 | 134211 | 134211 | 1333 | 32 1 | 2134 | 1114 (5fr)

G7 Cmaj7 Bm7 Am7 D7 E♭ Dm7 Em G7/D

131211 | 32 | 13121 | 2 1 | 213 | 1333 (6fr) | 211 | | 1

Intro |**Gmaj7** |**Fmaj7** |**Gmaj7** |**D** **F** |**G** **B♭** |

Verse 1

```
C                 Cm9       Am9
Spending my day   thinking 'bout you, girl.

Gmaj7  G7
   Being here with you, being near with you,

            C                Cm9  Am9          Gmaj7
I can't ex - plain myself why I        feel like I do.

        G7
Though it hurt me so to let you know.
```

Verse 2

```
      C                     Cm9
Oh, I look in your eyes and you let me know

Am9         Gmaj7      G7
   How you feel, let me know that love is really real.

      Cm9            Am9                   Cm9
But it seems to me that I'm wrapped up in your love.
```

Chorus 1

```
                                   Cmaj7  Bm7
Don't you know that I'm still in    love,

      Am7                D7  E♭  F G
Sho - nuff in love with you?

                              Cmaj7  Bm7
Well, I know that I'm still in    love

      Am7                D7  Dm7  Em  Dm7   Em  Dm7
Sho - nuff in love with you.
```

Verse 3

```
G7/D  C                     Cm9
When I look in your eyes, all the years
Am9     Gmaj7  G7
  How I see        me loving you and you loving me.
  Cm9                Am9                        Cm9
It seems to me that I'm wrapped up in your love.
```

Chorus 2

```
                                   Cmaj7  Bm7
Don't you know that I'm still in    love,

      Am7                D7
Sho - nuff in love with you?

     Cm9   Am9   Cm9
Hey, ___ I, ___ I, ___ don't you know that I'm

Cmaj7  Bm7        Am7              Bm7
Still in    love, sho - nuff in love with you?

       Cmaj7   Bm7           Am7  D7  Cm9  Am9
Hey, I try if you want me to.   I,   I,    I...
```

Fade out

If

Words and Music by David Gates

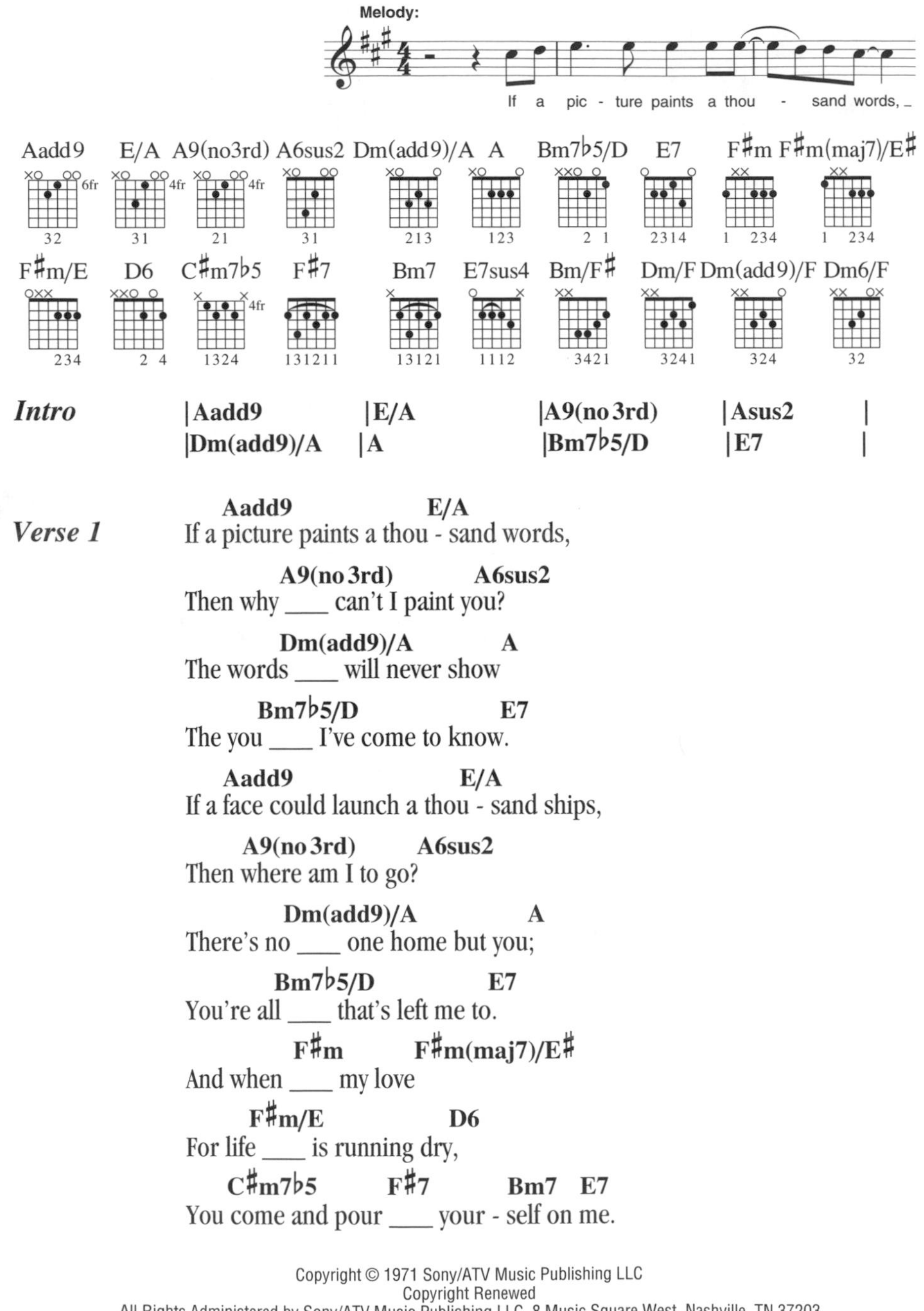

Intro

Aadd9	E/A	A9(no 3rd)	Asus2
Dm(add9)/A	A	Bm7♭5/D	E7

Verse 1

Aadd9 E/A
If a picture paints a thou - sand words,

A9(no 3rd) A6sus2
Then why ___ can't I paint you?

Dm(add9)/A A
The words ___ will never show

Bm7♭5/D E7
The you ___ I've come to know.

Aadd9 E/A
If a face could launch a thou - sand ships,

A9(no 3rd) A6sus2
Then where am I to go?

Dm(add9)/A A
There's no ___ one home but you;

Bm7♭5/D E7
You're all ___ that's left me to.

F♯m F♯m(maj7)/E♯
And when ___ my love

F♯m/E D6
For life ___ is running dry,

C♯m7♭5 F♯7 Bm7 E7
You come and pour ___ your - self on me.

Verse 2

```
    Aadd9                E/A             A9(no 3rd)
If a man could be two plac - es at one time,
             A6sus2  Dm(add9)/A   A
I'd be with you ___ tomor - row and today,
     Bm7♭5/D            E7
Beside ___ you all the way.
     Aadd9                  E/A
If the world should stop revolv - ing,
           A9(no 3rd)     A6sus2
Spinning slow - ly down to die,
       Dm(add9)/A        A
I'd spend ___ the end with you;
       Bm7♭5/D                   E7
And when ___ the world was through,
        F♯m       F♯m(maj7)/E♯
Then one ___ by one
      F♯m/E              D6
The stars ___ would all go out.
    C♯m7♭5  F♯7        Bm7
Then you and I ___ would simply
E7sus4 Aadd9 Bm/F♯ Dm/F Dm(add9)/F Dm6/F A
Fly a  -  way.
```

The Keeper of the Stars

Words and Music by Karen Staley,
Danny Mayo and Dickey Lee

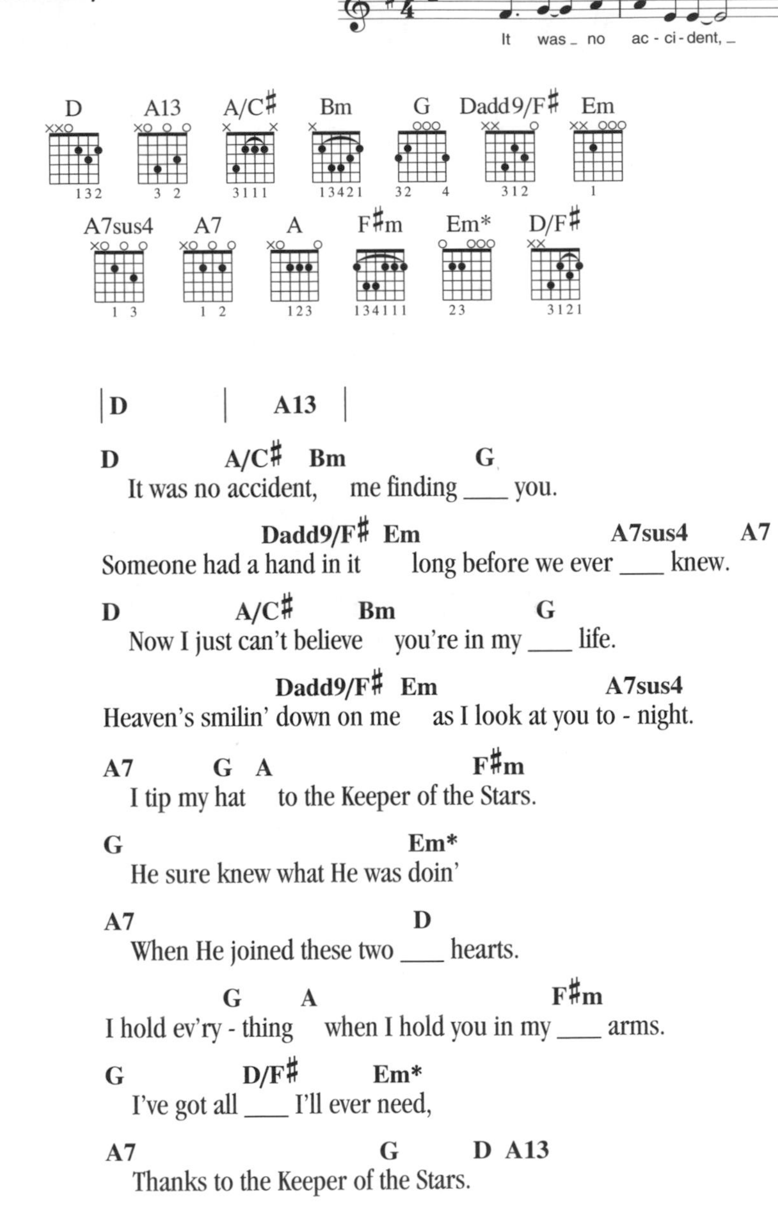

Intro | **D** | **A13** |

Verse 1

D A/C♯ Bm G
It was no accident, me finding ___ you.

Dadd9/F♯ Em A7sus4 A7
Someone had a hand in it long before we ever ___ knew.

D A/C♯ Bm G
Now I just can't believe you're in my ___ life.

Dadd9/F♯ Em A7sus4
Heaven's smilin' down on me as I look at you to - night.

Chorus 1

A7 G A F♯m
I tip my hat to the Keeper of the Stars.

G Em*
He sure knew what He was doin'

A7 D
When He joined these two ___ hearts.

G A F♯m
I hold ev'ry - thing when I hold you in my ___ arms.

G D/F♯ Em*
I've got all ___ I'll ever need,

A7 G D A13
Thanks to the Keeper of the Stars.

Verse 2

```
D                A/C#       Bm             G
  Soft moonlight on your face,   oh, how you ___ shine.
            Dadd9/F#       Em                  A7sus4    A7
It takes my ___ breath away   just to look into your ___ eyes.
D          A/C#        Bm            G
  I know I don't deserve   a treasure like ___ you.
                Dadd9/F#     Em              A7sus4
There really are ___ no words   to show my grati - tude.
```

Chorus 2

```
A7           G   A                   F#m
  So, I tip my hat   to the Keeper of the Stars.
G                         Em*
  He sure knew what He was doin'
A7                        D
  When He joined these two ___ hearts.
           G      A                    F#m
I hold ev'ry - thing   when I hold you in my ___ arms.
G        D/F#     Em*
  I've got all I'll ever need,
A7                        D
  Thanks to the Keeper of the Stars.
```

Outro

```
D          A/C#   Bm          G
  It was no accident,   me finding ___ you.
               Dadd9/F#
Someone had a hand in it
Em         A7              D  A13 D
  Long be - fore we ever knew.
```

Let's Stay Together

Words and Music by Al Green,
Willie Mitchell and Al Jackson, Jr.

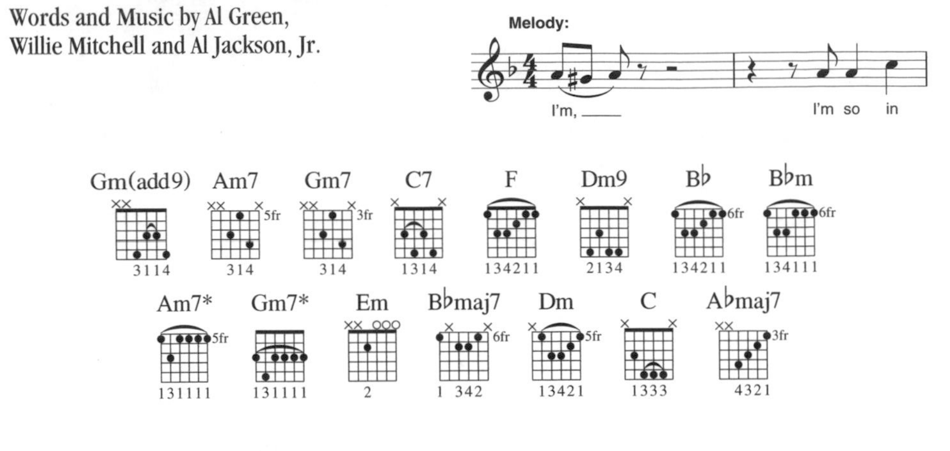

Intro **|Gm(add9) Am7 |Gm7 Am7 |Gm(add9) Am7 |Gm7 C7 |**

Verse 1

F Dm9
I'm, I'm so in love with you.

B♭ B♭m
Whatever you want to do, it's alright with me.

Am7* Gm7* F Em Dm9
'Cause you make me feel so brand-new,

Am7* Gm7* F Am7 Dm9
And I _______ want to spend my life with you.

Verse 2

F Dm9
Let me say since, baby, since we've been to - gether,

B♭ B♭m
Ooh, lovin' you for - ever is what I need.

Am7* Gm7* F Em Dm9
Let me be the one you come running to.

Am7* Gm7* F Am7* Dm9
I'll ______ never be un - true.

Chorus 1

```
             Gm(add9)      Am7
Ooh, baby, let's, let's stay together,

             Gm7                              B♭maj7   Am7
Loving you whether, whether times are good or bad,

   Dm        C      Gm(add9)  A♭maj7  Gm(add9)  A♭maj7
Hap - py or sad.

                     B♭maj7     Am7    Dm       C
Whether times are good or bad, ___ hap - py or sad.
```

Verse 3

```
F                           Dm9
Why, somebody, why people break up

                         B♭                  B♭m
Oh, an' turn around and make up I just can't see.

Am7*  Gm7*  F  Em   Dm9
You'd    never do that to me, would ya, baby.

Am7*     Gm7*     F     Am7*  Dm9
  So being   around you is all I    see.

It's why I want us to…
```

Outro-Chorus

```
    Gm(add9)                  Am7              Gm7
‖: Let's, we oughtta stay to - gether, loving you whether,

                           Am7  Gm7      C7
Whether times are good or bad, hap - py or sad.  :‖ Repeat and fade
```

Longer

Words and Music by
Dan Fogelberg

Melody:

Long - er than _ there've been fish - es in the o-cean,

Open G tuning:
(low to high) D–G–D–G–B–D

G Am11 Gmaj7/B Cadd9 G/B C Csus2

Bb Fadd9/C Ebadd9/Bb D7sus4/G D7/F# Dm7/F

Intro

G Am11	Gmaj7/B Cadd9	G Am11
G/B C	G Am11	G/B Csus2
Bb Am11	G	

Verse 1

```
G                  Am11                 Gmaj7/B    Cadd9
  Longer than ___ there've been fish - es in the o-cean,
G                  Am11 Gmaj7/B    Cadd9
  Higher than ___ any bird ever flew,
G                  Am11              Gmaj7/B          Cadd9
  Longer than ___ there've been stars up in the heav-ens,
Bb                 Am11      G
I've been in love ___ with you.
```

Verse 2

```
G                  Am11  Gmaj7/B       Cadd9
  Stronger than ___ any mountain cathe-dral,
G                 Am11 Gmaj7/B     Cadd9
  Truer than ___ any tree ever grew,
G                  Am11  Gmaj7/B    Cadd9
  Deeper than ___ any forest prime-val,
Bb            Am11      G
I am in love ___ with you.
```

```
              Fadd9/C  C     E♭add9/B♭   B♭
Chorus        I'll          bring fire in the win - ters.

              Fadd9/C  C    E♭add9/B♭          B♭
              You'll        send showers in the springs.

              Fadd9/C  C E♭add9/B♭          B♭
              We'll         fly through the falls and summers

                  D7sus4/G  D7/F♯       Dm7/F    D7/F♯
              With love _________ on our wings.

              G                       Am11        Gmaj7/B    Cadd9
Verse 3         Through the years ___ as the fire ___ starts to mellow,

              G           Am11             Gmaj7/B      Cadd9
                Burning lines in the book ___ of our lives,

                          G                 Am11             Gmaj7/B  Cadd9
              Though the binding cracks ___ and the pag - es start to yellow,

              B♭              Am11      G  B♭            Am11    G
              I'll be in love ___ with you.  I'll be in love ___ with you.

Trumpet Solo  ‖: Fadd9/C      C      | E♭add9/B♭    B♭     :‖ Play 3 times
              | D7sus4/G      D7/F♯ | Dm7/F     D7/F♯      |

              G               Am11               Gmaj7/B      Cadd9
Verse 4         Longer than ___ there've been fishes in the o - cean,

              G               Am11  Gmaj7/B     Cadd9
                Higher than ___ any bird ever flew,

              G               Am11               Gmaj7/B            Cadd9
                Longer than ___ there've been stars up in the heav - ens,

              B♭                 Am11      G  B♭            Am11     G
              I've been in love ___ with you.  I am in love ___ with you.
```

The Look of Love

from CASINO ROYALE

Words by Hal David
Music by Burt Bacharach

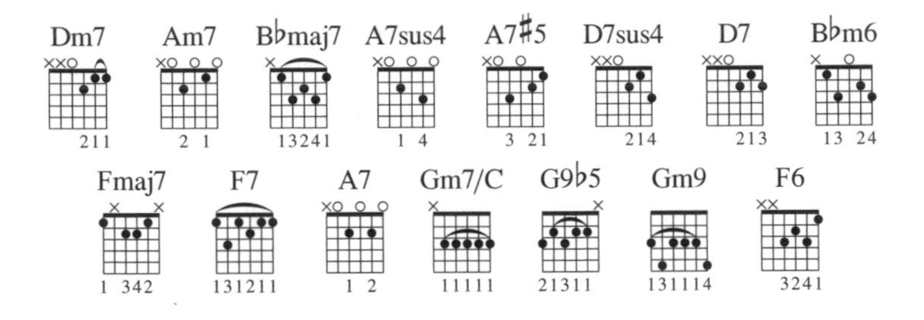

Verse 1

Dm7 Am7
The look ___ of love is in ___ your eyes,

B♭maj7 A7sus4
A look ___ your smile can't disguise.

A7♯5 Dm7 D7sus4 D7
The look ___ of love

B♭maj7 B♭m6
Is saying so ___ much more

Fmaj7 F7
Than just words could ever say.

B♭maj7 A7sus4 A7
And what my heart has heard, well, it takes my breath a - way.

Gm7/C Fmaj7 Gm7/C
I can hard - ly wait to hold you, feel ___ my arms around you,

Fmaj7 Gm7/C Fmaj7
How long I have waited, waited just to love you.

```
            Gm7/C                                   A7#5        Dm7
Verse 2   Now ___ that I have found you, you've got the look ___ of love,

               Am7                  Bbmaj7                 A7sus4
          It's on ___ your face, a look ___ that time can't erase.

          A7#5      Dm7        D7sus4  D7
            Be mine ___ tonight,

          Bbmaj7           Bbm6
            Let this be just ___ the start

                                 Fmaj7  F7
          Of so many nights like this.

          Bbmaj7                               A7sus4      A7
            Let's take a lover's vow and then seal it with a kiss.

          Gm7/C     Fmaj7                      Gm7/C
            I can hard - ly wait to hold you, feel ___ my arms around you,

          Fmaj7               Gm7/C  Fmaj7
            How long I have waited,  waited just to love you.

             Gm7/C                           A7#5      Dm7         G9b5
          Now ___ that I have found you don't ever go, don't ever go.

          Gm9  Gm7/C     F6
                    I love you so.
```

Love Without End, Amen

Words and Music by Aaron G. Barker

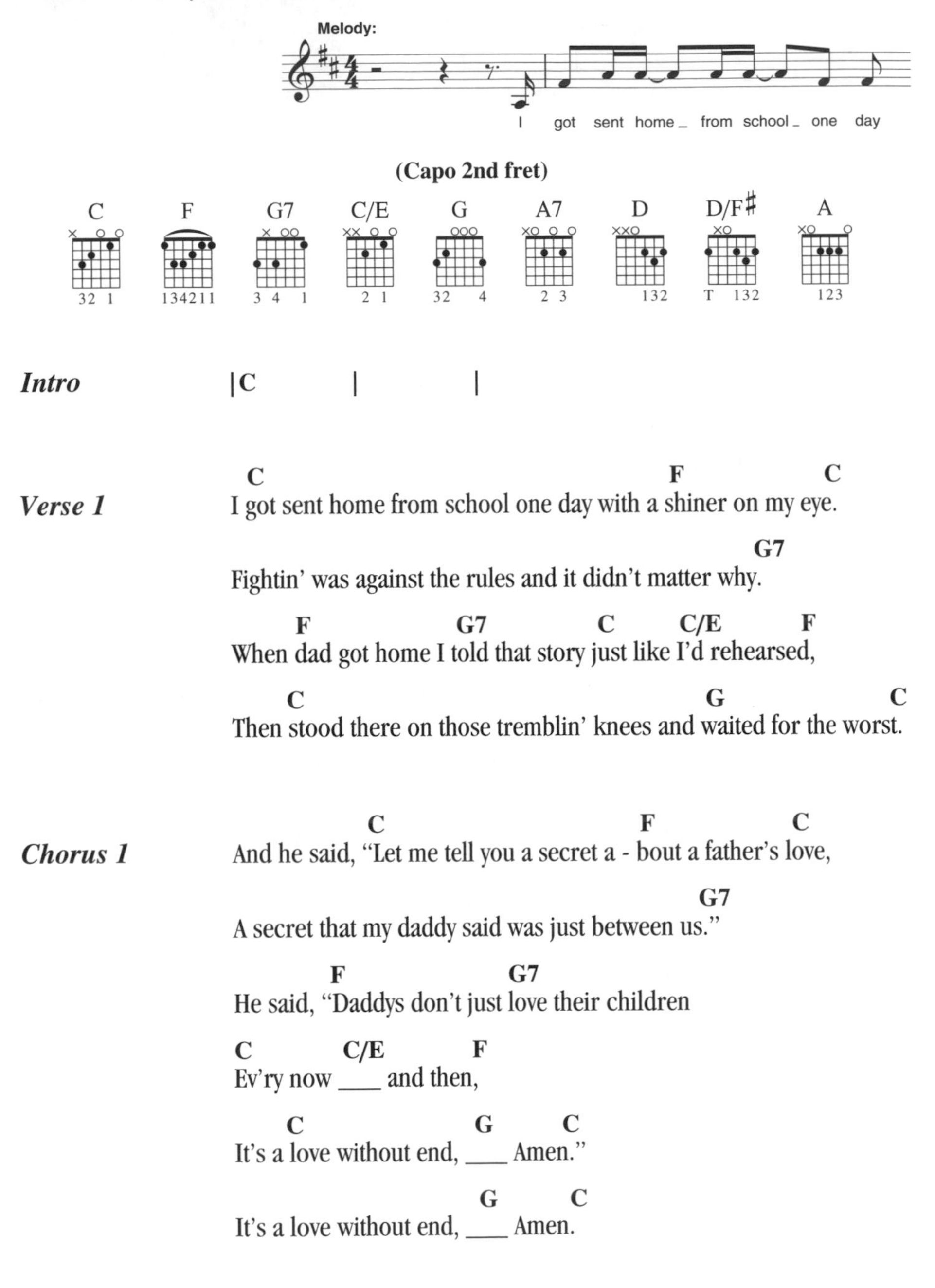

Intro |C | |

Verse 1

C I got sent home from school one day with a **F** shiner on my **C** eye.
Fightin' was against the rules and it didn't matter **G7** why.
When **F** dad got home I **G7** told that story **C** just like **C/E** I'd rehearsed, **F**
Then **C** stood there on those tremblin' knees and **G** waited for the **C** worst.

Chorus 1

And he said, "**C** Let me tell you a secret a - **F** bout a father's **C** love,
A secret that my daddy said was just between **G7** us."
He said, "**F** Daddys don't just **G7** love their children
C Ev'ry now **C/E** ___ and **F** then,
It's a **C** love without end, **G** ___ Amen." **C**
It's a love without end, **G** ___ Amen. **C**

Verse 2

```
       C                         F                    C
When I became a father in the spring of eighty-one
                                                                G7
There was no doubt that stubborn boy was just like my father's son.
    F                   G7                     C      C/E    F
And when I thought my patience had been tested to the end,
 C                             G                C
I took my daddy's secret and I passed it on to him.
```

Chorus 2

```
          C                          F            C
I said, "Let me tell you a secret a - bout a father's love,
                                                  G7
A secret that my daddy said was just between us."
          F                 G7
I said, "Daddys don't just love their children
C          C/E          F
Ev'ry now ___ and then,
        C                        G        C
It's a love without end, ___ Amen."
                                 G        C
It's a love without end, ___ Amen.
```

Verse 3

```
A7     D                                                   G                 D
   Last night I dreamed I died and stood outside ___ those pearly gates.
                                                                A7
When suddenly, I realized there must be some mistake.
  G                              A7                       D        D/F#       G
If they know half the things ___ I've done they'll never let ___ me in.
              D                                     A7                     D
And then somewhere from the other side I heard these words again.
```

Chorus 3

```
                       D                            G                D
And they said, "Let me tell you a secret a - bout a father's love,
                                                   A7
A secret that my daddy said was just between us."
              G                 A
You see "Daddys just don't love their children
D          D/F#         G
Ev'ry now ___ and then,
        D                        A        D
It's a love without end, ___ Amen."
                                 A        D
It's a love without end, ___ Amen.
```

Love's Grown Deep

Words and Music by Kenny Nolan

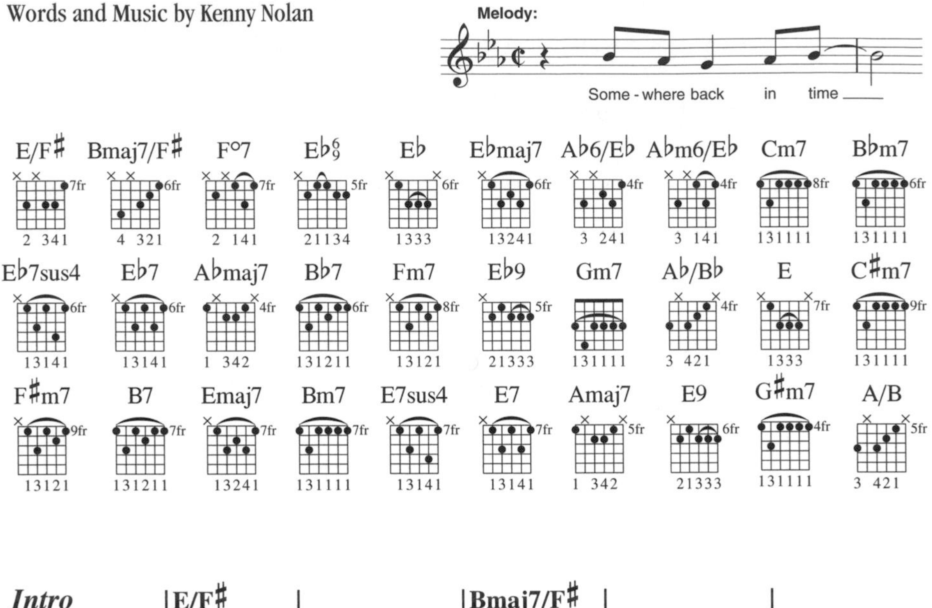

Intro

E/F♯		Bmaj7/F♯	*I love you*
F°7	*So much.*	E♭6/9	

Verse 1

```
Eb                        Ebmaj7      Ab6/Eb
  Somewhere back in time you be - came a friend of mine,
Ebmaj7                                   Ab6/Eb
  And day by day we've grown a little closer.
          Eb       Ebmaj7  Ab6/Eb
You're my spirit to be strong, a friend when things go wrong,
Abm6/Eb Eb                        Cm7          Bbm7 Eb7sus4 Eb7
  So I've written down these words ___ to let you know.
```

Chorus 1

A♭maj7 B♭7 E♭maj7
Love's grown deep, deep into the heart of me,

Cm7 Fm7
You've become a part of me,

B♭7 E♭maj7 E♭9
Let us plant the seed and watch it grow.

A♭maj7 B♭7 Gm7
Love's grown deep, deep into the heart of me,

Cm7 A♭/B♭
You've become a part of me.

Verse 2

E♭ Cm7
As we travel down the road

Fm7 B♭7
Side ____ by side we'll share the load.

E♭maj7 Cm7 Fm7
Hand in hand we'll see each other through.

B♭7 E♭ Cm7
Though we've only just begun,

Fm7 B♭7
Let's count our blessings one by one.

E♭maj7 Cm7 B♭m7 E♭7sus4 E♭7
I thank God for life, I thank God for you.

Chorus 2

Repeat Chorus 1

Harmonica Solo

| E | C♯m7 | F♯m7 | B7 |
| Emaj7 | C♯m7 | F♯m7 | B7 |

Verse 3

```
                E                     C#m7
And as the seasons slip away,

              F#m7                  B7
Forever lover's we will stay,

      Emaj7           C#m7                              Bm7  E7sus4  E7
To - gether do or die ___ with all our heart.
```

Chorus 3

```
Amaj7                 B7                             Emaj7
Love's grown deep, deep into the heart of me,

C#m7                                F#m7
You've become a part of me,

B7                                Emaj7     E9
Let us plant the seed and      watch it grow.

Amaj7                  B7                     G#m7
Love's grown deep, deep into the heart ___ of me,

C#m7                               A/B
You've become a part of me.
```

Outro

```
     Amaj7  G#m7  F#m7             Emaj7
||: Ah,         ah,       ah, whew, ooh, ooh.

Amaj7  G#m7  A/B    B7
Ah,        ah, ah.                    :||
```

Repeat and fade

More Than Words

Words and Music by
Nuno Bettencourt and Gary Cherone

Melody:

Say-ing "I ___ love ___ you"

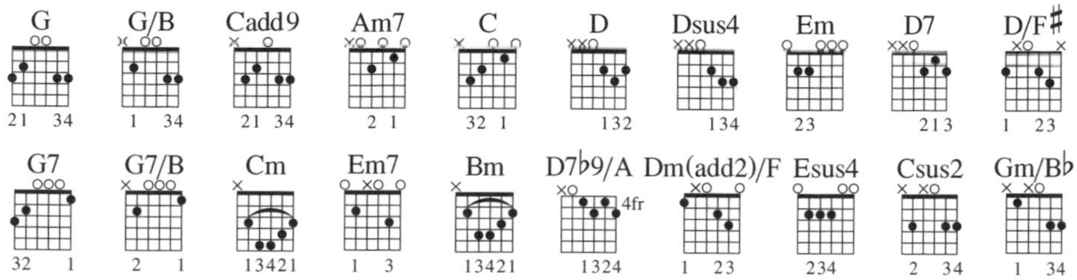

G G/B Cadd9 Am7 C D Dsus4 Em D7 D/F♯

21 34 | 1 34 | 21 34 | 2 1 | 32 1 | 132 | 134 | 23 | 213 | 1 23

G7 G7/B Cm Em7 Bm D7♭9/A Dm(add2)/F Esus4 Csus2 Gm/B♭

32 1 | 2 1 | 13421 | 1 3 | 13421 | 4fr 1324 | 1 23 | 234 | 2 34 | 1 34

Intro ‖: G G/B Cadd9 | Am7 | C | D Dsus4 G :‖

Verse 1

G G/B Cadd9
Sayin', "I love you"

Am7 C D Dsus4 G
Is not the words I want to hear from you.

G/B Cadd9 Am7
It's not that I want you not to say,

C D Dsus4 Em Am7 D7
But if you on - ly knew how easy it would be,

G D/F♯ Em
To show me how you feel.

Chorus 1

Am7 D7 G7 G7/B C
More than words is all you have to do to make it real.

Cm G Em
Then you wouldn't have to say that you love me,

Am7 D7 G
'Cause I'd al - ready know.

D/F♯ Em Bm C
What would you do___ if my heart was torn in two?

G/B Am7
More than words to show you feel

D7 G
That your love for me is real.

D/F♯ Em Bm C
What would you say__ if I took those words a-way?

G/B Am7
Then you couldn't make things new

D7 G
Just by say - in', "I love you."

Interlude

G G/B Cadd9 Am7
La, dee, da , la, dee, da,

C
Dee, dai, dai, da.

D Dsus4 G G/B Cadd9
More than words.

Am7 D7
La, dee, da, dai, da.

Verse 2

G G/B Cadd9 Am7
Now that I've tried to talk to you

C D Dsus4 G
And make you un - der - stand,

G/B Cadd9 Am7
All you__ have to do is close your eyes

C D Dsus4 Em
And just reach out your hands

Am7 D7 G D/F♯ Em
And__ touch me, hold me close, don't ever let me go.

Chorus 2

Am7 D7 G7 G7/B C
More than words is all I ever needed you__ to show.

Cm G
Then you wouldn't have to say

Em
That you love me,

Am7 D D7♭9/A G
'Cause I'd al - read - y know.

D/F♯
What would you do

Em Bm C
If my heart was torn in two?

G/B Am7
More than words to show you feel

D7 G
That your love for me is real.

D/F♯
What would you say

Em Bm C
If I took those words a-way?

G/B Am7
Then you couldn't make things new

D7 G G/B Cadd9
Just by say - ing "I love you."

Outro

Am7
‖: La, dee, da, dai, dai,

C
Dee, dai, dai, da.

D Dsus4 G G/B Cadd9
More than words. :‖ ***Play 3 times***

Am7
La, dee, da, dai, dai,

C
Dee, dai, dai, da.

D Dsus4 G D/F♯
More than words.

Dm(add9)/F Esus4
Oo, oo, oo, oo,

Am7 D
Oo, oo, oo.

N.C. G Csus2 G/B Gm/B♭ Am7 G
More than words.

Loving You

Words and Music by
Jerry Leiber and Mike Stoller

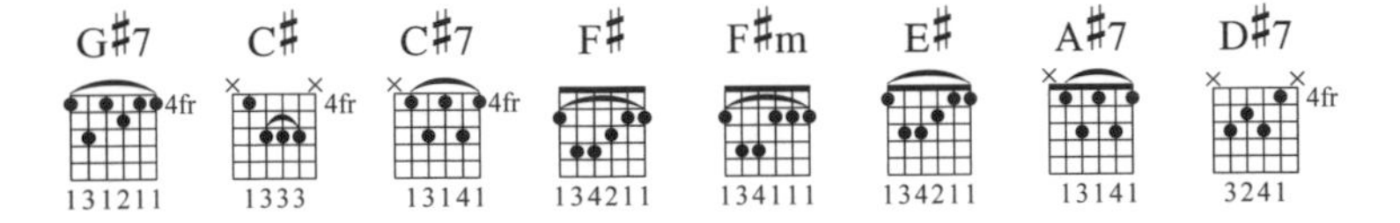

Intro | G♯7 |

Verse 1

C♯
I will spend my whole life through
G♯7
Loving you, just loving you.

Winter, summer, springtime, too.
C♯ C♯7
Loving you, loving you.
F♯ F♯m
Makes no diff'rence where I go
C♯ E♯ A♯7
Or what I may do.
D♯7
You know that I'll always be
G♯7 D♯7 G♯7
Lov - ing you, just you and

Verse 2

```
C#
   If I'm seen with someone new,
G#7
   Don't be blue, don't you be blue.

I'll be faithful, I'll be true.
C#                          C#7
   Always true, true to you.
F#                   F#m
   There is only one for me,
    C# E#   A#7
And you know who.
D#7
   You know that I'll always be
G#7   C#
Loving you.
```

More
(Ti Guarderò Nel Cuore)
from the film MONDO CANE

Music by Nino Oliviero and Riz Ortolani
Italian Lyrics by Marcello Ciorciolini
English Lyrics by Norman Newell

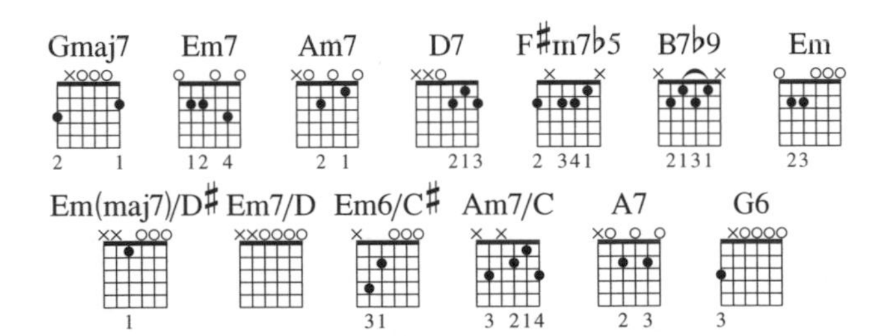

Verse 1

Gmaj7 Em7 Am7 D7
More than the greatest love the world has known,
Gmaj7 Em7 Am7 D7
This is the love I'll give you a - lone.
Gmaj7 Em7 Am7 D7
More than the simple words I try to say,
Gmaj7 Em7 Am7 F♯m7♭5 B7♭9
I only live to love you more each day.

Chorus 1

Em Em(maj7)/D♯
More than you'll ever know,
Em7/D Em6/C♯
My arms long to hold you so.
Am7/C A7
My life will be in your keeping,
Am7 D7
Waking, sleeping, laughing, weeping.

Verse 2

Gmaj7 Em7 Am7 D7
Longer than always is a long, long time

Gmaj7 Em7 Am7 F#m7b5 B7b9
But far be - yond forever you'll be mine.

Chorus 2

Em Em(maj7)/D#
I know I never lived

Em7/D Em6/C# Am7/C
Be - fore and my heart is very sure

Am7 D7 G6
No one else could love you more.

My Heart Will Go On

(Love Theme from 'Titanic')

from the Paramount and Twentieth Century Fox Motion Picture TITANIC

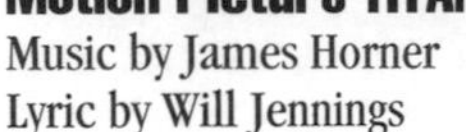
Music by James Horner
Lyric by Will Jennings

C♯m7 Bsus4 A B E Bsus4/F♯ Esus4 Asus2

E/B C♯m Badd4 G♯m G♯7/B♯ G♯7 Fm E♭

D♭ E♭sus4 Cm7 A♭/E♭ A♭ E♭/A♭ D♭/A♭

Intro ‖: **C♯m7** | **Bsus4** | **A** | **Bsus4** **B** :‖

Verse 1

```
E                Bsus4/F#    Esus4
Ev'ry night in my dreams I see you,
  E   B    E            Bsus4/F#    A
I feel you, that is how I know you go on.
E               B              Asus2        E/B  B
Far across the distance and spaces be - tween us,
E                 B            Asus2
You have come to show you go on.
```

Chorus 1

```
C#m  Badd4     A           B
Near,  far, wher - ever you are,
       C#m          B                A  B
I be - lieve that the heart does go on.
C#m  B           A           B
Once  more you open the door
              C#m        G#m
And you're here in my heart,
          A              E/B  B    C#m7  Bsus4  A  Bsus4  B
And my heart will go on     and on.
```

Verse 2

E B Asus2 E/B B
Love can touch us one time and last for a life - time,

E B Asus2
And never let go till we're gone.

E B Asus2 E/B G#7/B#
Love was when I loved you, one true time I'd hold to.

C#m G#m Asus2
In my life we'll always go on.

Chorus 2

C#m Badd4 A B
Near, far, wher - ever you are,

C#m B A B
I believe ___ that the heart does go on.

C#m B A B
Once more you open the door

C#m G#m
And you're here in my heart,

A E/B B C#m7 Bsus4 A Bsus4 B
And my heart will go on and on.

| C#m7 | Bsus4 | A | C#m G#7 |

Outro-Chorus

Fm Eb Db Eb
You're here, there's nothing I fear

Fm Eb Db Ebsus4 Eb
And I know ___ that my heart ___ will go on.

Fm Eb Db Eb
We'll stay for - ever this way.

Fm Cm7
You are safe ___ in my heart,

Db Ab/Eb Eb Ab Eb/Ab Db/Ab
And my heart will go on and on.

Eb/Ab Ab Eb/Ab Db/Ab Ab
Mm.

Never My Love

Words and Music by Don Addrisi
and Dick Addrisi

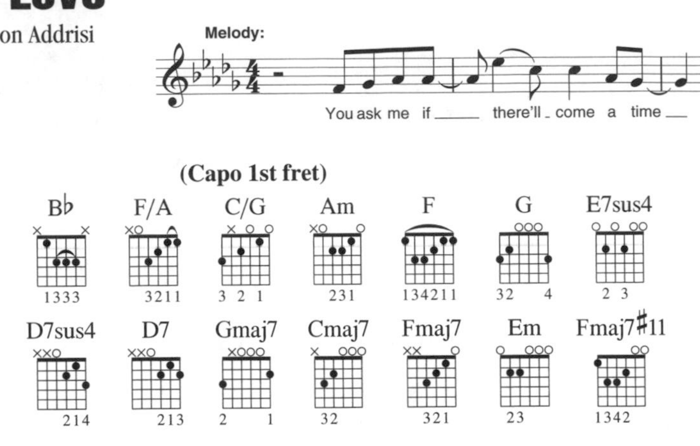

Intro

N.C. |C | N.C. |C | N.C. |

Verse 1

```
C                    G/B                  B♭
   You ask me if ___ there'll come a time
                      F/A       C/G
When I grow tired ___ of you,
Am                 C     F              C
   Never my love, ___    never my love.
                  G                     B♭
You wonder if ___ this heart of mine
                        F         C
Will lose its desire ___ for you,
Am                 C     F              C
   Never my love, ___    never my love.
```

Bridge 1

```
E7sus4 E7                Am7           D7sus4 D7
       What makes you think love will end

            Gmaj7        Cmaj7         Fmaj7  Em        Am N.C.
When you know that my whole life de - pends on you? (On you.)
```

Verse 2

```
C               G               B♭
  Da, da, da, da, ___ da, da, da, da.

        F        C
Da, da, da, da, da, da, da.

Am              C   F           C
  Never my love, ___   never my love.

               G                B♭
You say you fear ___ I'll change my mind,

               F  C
I won't require ___ you,

Am              C   F           C
  Never my love, ___   never my love.
```

Bridge 2

```
E7sus4 E7              Am7          D7sus4 D7
       How can you think love will end

            Gmaj7       Cmaj7            Fmaj7  Em
When I've asked you to spend your whole life with me?

      Fmaj7♯11
(With me. With me.)
```

Outro-
Organ Solo

```
‖: C        | G        | B♭        | F    C    |

Am              C                F
  Never my love, ___ (Never my love.)

                C
Never my love. :‖  Repeat and fade
```

The One That You Love

Words and Music by Graham Russell

Melody:

Now the night___ has gone,

C Gm Dm Bm7♭5 Em7♭5/B♭ A7/C♯ Dm/C G G/F G/C

F/C A/C♯ B♭ F Dm7 B♭maj7 C7sus4 C/F B♭/F

Intro | C | |

Verse 1

C **Gm**
Now the night has gone, now the night has gone a - way.

C **Gm**
Doesn't seem that long, we hardly had two words to say.

Dm **Bm7♭5**
Hold me in your arms for just an - other day,

C **Em7♭5/B♭** **A7/C♯**
I promise this one will go slow, oh,

Dm **Dm/C** **G**
We have the right you know,

Dm **Dm/C** **G**
We have the right you know.

Verse 2

```
C                                                              Gm
Don't say the morning's come, don't say the morning's come so soon.

C                                                    Gm
Must we end this way, when so much here is hard to lose?

Dm                     Bm7b5
Love is ev'rywhere, I know it is.

     C            Em7b5/Bb  A7/C#
Such moments as this are too  few, oh.

Dm       Dm/C  G
  It's all up to  you,

Dm       Dm/C  G
  It's all up to  you.
```

Chorus 1

```
G/F      C                     G/C
  Here I am, the one that you love,

               F/C    G/C
Asking for an - other day.

        C                       G/C
Under - stand, the one that you love,

               F/C      G/C  F/C
Loves you in so many ways.
```

Verse 3

```
C                                          Gm
Tell me we can stay, tell me we can stay, oh, please.

C                                                     Gm
They are the words to say, the only words I can be - lieve.

Dm                                    Bm7b5
Hold me in your arms for just an - other day,

  C              Em7b5/Bb  A7/C#
I promise this one will go  slow, oh,

Dm              Dm/C    G
  We have the right you know,

Dm              Dm/C    G
  We have the right you know.
```

Chorus 2

```
G/F        C                          G/C
   Here I am, the one that you love,

                  F/C      G/C
Asking for an - other day.

         C                            G/C
Under - stand, the one that you love,

                  F/C       G/C
Loves you in so many ways.

       C                         G/C
Here I am, the one that you love,

                  F/C      G/C
Asking for an - other day.

         C                            G/C
Under - stand, the one that you love,

                  F/C       G/C
Loves you in so many ways.
```

Bridge

```
A/C♯                                       Dm  Dm/C
   The night has gone, a part of yester - day.

B♭                        F   Dm7                      B♭maj7  C7sus4
   I don't know what to say, ____ I don't know what to say.
```

Outro-Chorus

```
                  F                        C/F
‖:  Here I am, the one that you love,

                  B♭/F     C/F
Asking for an - other day.

          F                          C/F
Under - stand the one that you love,

                  B♭/F      C/F
Loves you in so many ways.        :‖  Repeat and fade
```

(You're My) Soul and Inspiration

Words and Music by
Barry Mann and Cynthia Weil

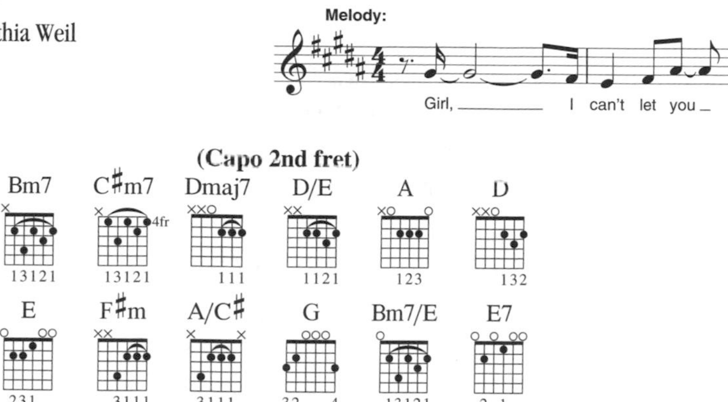

Verse 1

Bm7 C♯m7
Girl, I can't let you do this,
Dmaj7 C♯m7
Let you walk away.
Bm7 C♯m7
Girl, how can I live through this
Dmaj7 D/E
When you're all I wake up for each day?

Chorus 1

A D E
Baby, you're my soul and my ___ inspi - ration.
A D E
You're all I've got to get me by.
A D E
You're my soul and my ___ inspi - ration.
F♯m E D A/C♯ G Bm7/E E7
With - out you, ba - by, what good am I?

Verse 2

Bm7 C#m7
I never had much goin',

Dmaj7 C#m7
But at least I had you.

Bm7 C#m7
How can you walk out knowin'

Dmaj7 D/E
I ain't got nothin' left if you do?

Chorus 2

A D E
Baby, you're my soul and my ___ inspi - ration.

A D E
You're all I've got to get me by.

A D E
You're my soul and my ___ inspi - ration.

F#m E D A/C# G
With - out you, ba - by, what good am I?

Bm7/E E7 A D E D A D E D
Oh, what good am ___ I?

Bridge

A D E D A
(*Spoken:*) *Baby, I can't make it with - out you,*

D E D A
And I'm, I'm tellin' you honey,

D E D A
You're my reason for laughin',

D E D
For cryin', for livin' and for dyin'.

Verse 3

```
A    D E       D           A    D
Baby,    I can't make it with - out you.

E          D         A   D
   Please, I'm beggin' you, baby.

E          D          A
   If you go, ___ it will kill ___ me,

 D            D/E
I swear it, girl. My love can't bear it.
```

Chorus 3

```
A                      D       E
You're my soul and my ___ inspi - ration.

A                    D     E
   You're all I've got to get me by.

A                        D       E
   You're my soul and my ___ inspi - ration.

     F#m E   D  A/C#  G
With - out  you, ba - by, what good am I?

Bm7/E     E7   A      D E D
   What good am ___ I?
```

Outro ||: A D | E D :|| *Repeat and fade w/vocal ad lib*

The Power of Love

Words by Mary Susan Applegate and Jennifer Rush
Music by Candy Derouge and Gunther Mende

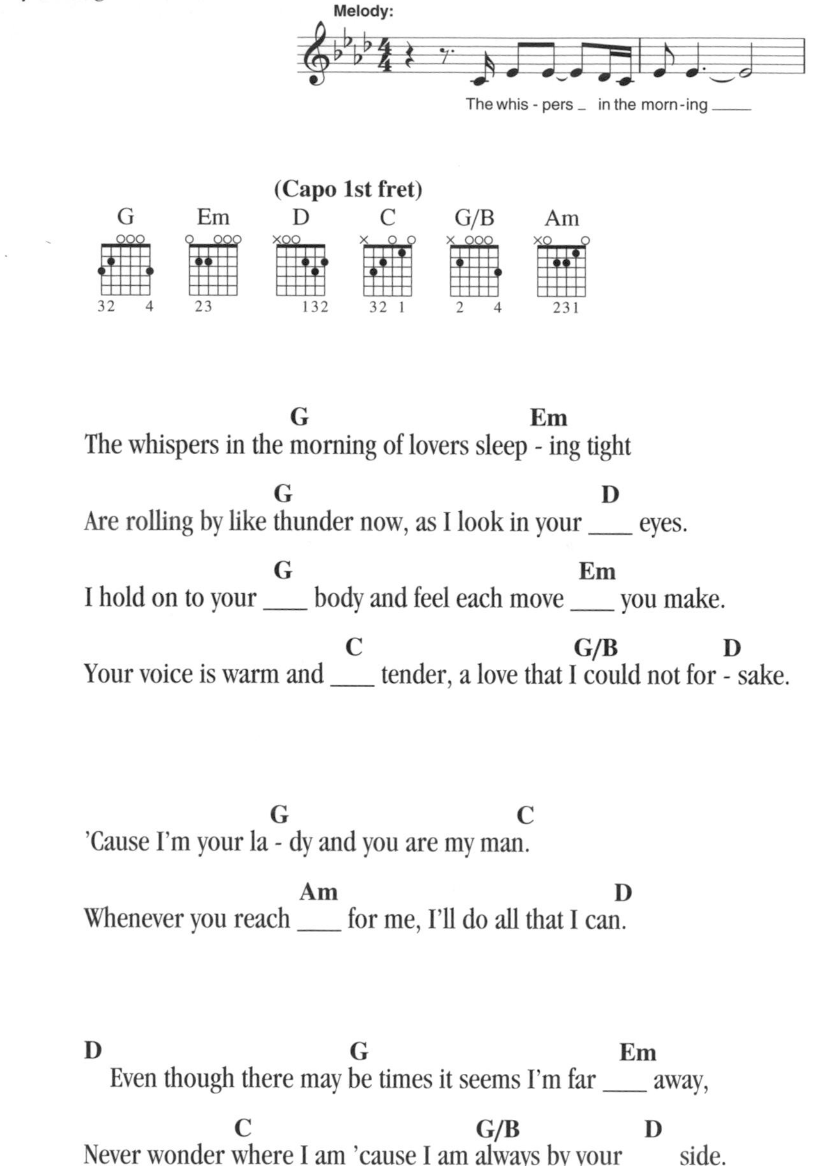

Verse 1

G Em
The whispers in the morning of lovers sleep - ing tight

G D
Are rolling by like thunder now, as I look in your ___ eyes.

G Em
I hold on to your ___ body and feel each move ___ you make.

C G/B D
Your voice is warm and ___ tender, a love that I could not for - sake.

Chorus 1

G C
'Cause I'm your la - dy and you are my man.

Am D
Whenever you reach ___ for me, I'll do all that I can.

Verse 2

D G Em
Even though there may be times it seems I'm far ___ away,

C G/B D
Never wonder where I am 'cause I am always by your ___ side.

```
                          G                              C
Chorus 2    'Cause I'm your la - dy and you are my man.

                              Am                                 D
            Whenever you reach ___ for me, I'll do all that I can.

                          G                                        C
            We're heading for something, somewhere I've never been.

                                Am                           D
            Sometimes I am fright - ened, but I'm ready to learn

                       C          G
            'Bout the power of love.


            C    D                  G
Bridge        The sound of your heart beating

            C       D           Em
              Made it clear sudden - ly.

            C    D          G
              The feeling that I can't go on

            C                   D  C  D
              Is light-years away.


            D C     D       G                           C
Chorus 3      'Cause I'm your la - dy and you are my man.

                             Am                                          D
            Whenever you reach ___ for me, I'm gonna do all that I can.

                          G                                        C
            We're heading for something, somewhere I've never been.

                                Am                           D
            Sometimes I am fright - ened, but I'm ready to learn

                       C             G
            'Bout the power of love. ___ The power of love.
```

Precious and Few

Words and Music by Walter D. Nims

Melody:

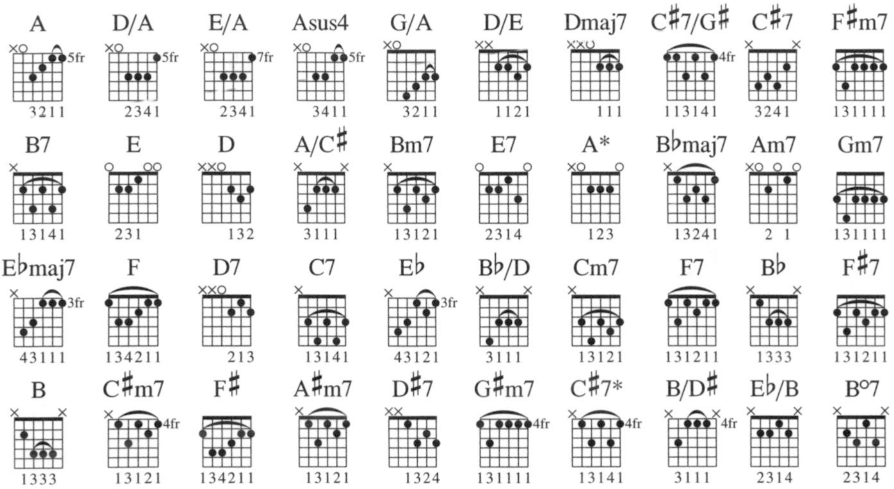

Pre-cious and few ___ are the mo - ments we

A 3211 · D/A 2341 · E/A 2341 · Asus4 3411 · G/A 3211 · D/E 1121 · Dmaj7 111 · C♯7/G♯ 113141 · C♯7 3241 · F♯m7 131111

B7 13141 · E 231 · D 132 · A/C♯ 3111 · Bm7 13121 · E7 2314 · A* 123 · B♭maj7 13241 · Am7 2 1 · Gm7 131111

E♭maj7 43111 · F 134211 · D7 213 · C7 13141 · E♭ 43121 · B♭/D 3111 · Cm7 13121 · F7 131211 · B♭ 1333 · F♯7 131211

B 1333 · C♯m7 13121 · F♯ 134211 · A♯m7 13121 · D♯7 1324 · G♯m7 131111 · C♯7* 13141 · B/D♯ 3111 · E♭/B 2314 · B°7 2314

Intro |**A** |**D/A** |**E/A** |**D/A** |

Verse 1

A **Asus4** **G/A** **Asus4**
Precious and few are the mo - ments we two can share.

A **Asus4** **G/A**
Quiet and blue like the sky ____ I'm hung over you.

D/E **Dmaj7** **C♯7/G♯** **C♯7**
And if I can't find my way back home,

F♯m7 **B7** **E**
It just wouldn't be fair,

D **A/C♯**
Precious and few

Bm7 **E7** **A*** **E7**
Are the mo - ments we two can share.

Verse 2

A Asus4 G/A Asus4
Baby, it's you on my mind, ___ your love is so rare.

A Asus4 G/A
Being with you is like a feel - ing I just can't com - pare.

D/E Dmaj7 C♯7/G♯ C♯7
And if I can't hold you in my arms,

F♯m7 B7 E
It just wouldn't be fair,

D A/C♯
'Cause precious and few

Bm7 E7 A*
Are the mo - ments we two can share.

Interlude

| B♭maj7 | Am7 | Gm7 E♭maj7 | F |

Verse 3

E♭maj7 Am7 D7
And if I can't find my way back home

Gm7 C7 F
It just wouldn't be fair,

E♭ B♭/D
'Cause precious and few

Cm7 F7 B♭ F♯7
Are the mo - ments we two can ___ share.

Verse 4

B C♯m7 A* F♯
Precious and few are the mo - ments we two can share.

B C♯m7 A* F♯
Quiet and blue like the sky ___ I'm hung over you.

E A♯m7 D♯7
And if I can't find my way back home,

G♯m7 C♯7* F♯
It just wouldn't be fair,

E B/D♯
'Cause precious and few

C♯m7 F♯7 E
Are the mo - ments we two can __ share.

B/D♯
(Precious and few

C♯m7 F♯7 B E6/B B°7 B
Are the moments we two ___ can share.)

Sometimes When We Touch

Words by Dan Hill
Music by Barry Mann

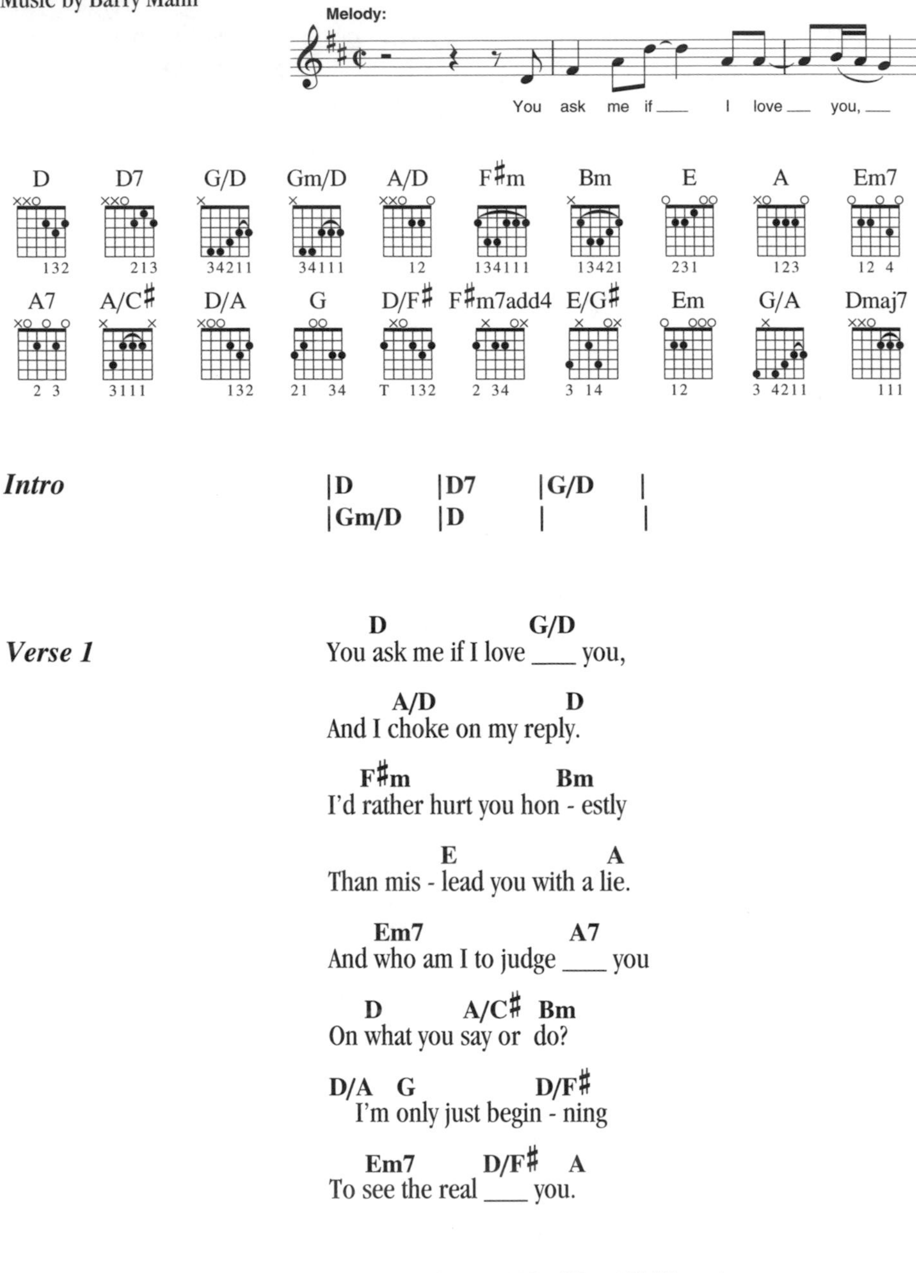

Intro

|D |D7 |G/D |
|Gm/D |D | |

Verse 1

D G/D
You ask me if I love ___ you,

A/D D
And I choke on my reply.

F#m Bm
I'd rather hurt you hon - estly

E A
Than mis - lead you with a lie.

Em7 A7
And who am I to judge ___ you

D A/C# Bm
On what you say or do?

D/A G D/F#
I'm only just begin - ning

Em7 D/F# A
To see the real ___ you.

Chorus 1

D G
And sometimes when we touch,

A F#m
The honesty's too much.

Bm E
And I have ___ to close my eyes

F#m7add4 E/G# A G
And ___________ hide.

F#m Em D G
I wanna hold you till I die,

A F#m
Till we both ___ break down and cry.

Em7 G/A D D7 G/D Gm/D
I wanna hold you till the fear ___ in me subsides.

Verse 2

D G/D
Ro - mance and all its strat - egy

A/D D
Leaves me battling with my pride.

F#m Bm
But through the insecur - ity

E A
Some tenderness survives.

Em7 A7
I'm just another writ - er

D A/C# Bm
Still trapped with - in my truth.

D/A G D/F#
A hesitant prizefight - er

Em7 D/F# A
Still trapped within ___ my youth.

Chorus 2

```
    D                            G
And sometimes when we touch,

    A                    F#m
The honesty's too much.

             Bm                 E
And I have ___ to close my eyes

F#m7(add4)  E/G#  A   G
And ___________  hide.

F#m  Em        D              G
         I wanna hold you till I die,

          A                          F#m
Till we both ___ break down and cry.

      Em7                 G/A                D
I wanna hold you till the fear ___ in me subsides.
```

Bridge

```
  G/D                                                 Dmaj7
At times I'd like to break you and drive you to your knees.

  Bm                   F#m                 G              G/A
At times I'd like to break ___ through and hold ___ you endlessly.
```

Verse 3

```
  D                  G/D
At times I understand ___ you,

     A/D                   D
And I know how hard you've tried.

   F#m                            Bm
I've watched while love commands ___ you,

           E                 A
And I've watched love pass you by.

  Em7                  A7
At times I think we're drift - ers,

   D          A/C#  Bm
Still searching for a  friend,

D/A  G          D/F#
   A brother or a sis - ter,

            Em7    D/F#    A
But then the passion flares a - gain.
```

Chorus 3

```
       D                           G
And sometimes when we touch,

       A                       F#m
The honesty's too much.

             Bm                        E
And I have ___ to close my eyes

F#m7(add4)  E/G#  A    G
And ___________ hide.

F#m  Em          D                     G
           I wanna hold you till I die,

                A                            F#m
Till we both ___ break down and cry.

          Em7                     G/A                  D   A/D  G/D  D
I wanna hold you till the fear ___ in me subsides.
```

Speak Softly Love (Love Theme)

from the Paramount Picture THE GODFATHER

Words by Larry Kusik
Music by Nino Rota

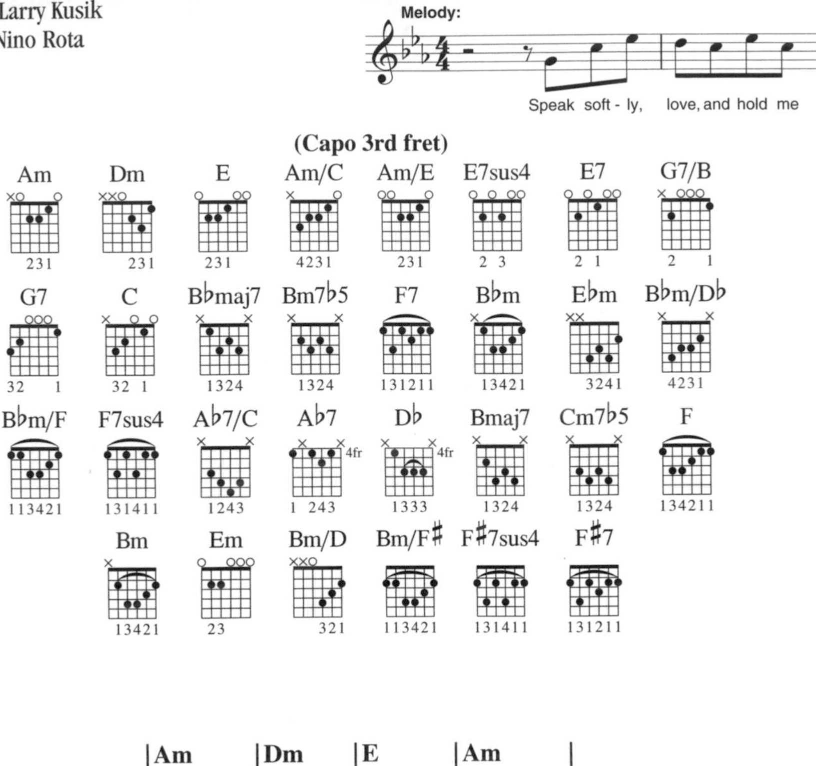

Intro |**Am** |**Dm** |**E** |**Am** |

Verse 1

Am Dm Am
Speak softly, love, and hold me warm against your heart.

Am/C Dm
I feel your words, the tender, trembling moments start.

Am
We're in a world our very own,

Am/E E7sus4 E7 Am
Sharing a love that only few have ever known.

Bridge 1

```
              G7/B  G7            C
Wine colored days   warmed by the sun,

            B♭maj7 Bm7♭5       E7sus4  E
Deep velvet nights   when we are one.
```

Verse 2

```
              Am              Dm                Am
Speak softly, love, so no one hears us but the sky.

                                    Am/C      Dm
The vows of love we make will live until we die.

                                Am
My life is yours and all be - cause

               Am/E               E7sus4  E7   Am            F7
You came in - to my world with love           so softly, love.
```

Instrumental

```
|B♭m   E♭m  |B♭m        |     B♭m/D♭      |E♭m      |
|           |B♭m        |B♭m/F  F7sus4  F7 |B♭m      |
```

Bridge 2

```
              A♭7/C  A♭7          D♭
Wine colored days   warmed by the sun,

            Bmaj7  Cm7♭5        F
Deep velvet nights    when we are one.
```

Verse 3

```
N.C.          Bm              Em                Bm
  Speak softly, love, so no one hears us but the sky.

                                    Bm/D      Em
The vows of love we make will live until we die.

                                Bm
My life is yours and all be - cause

               Bm/F♯              F♯7sus4  F♯7     Bm  Em  F♯7  Bm
You came in - to my world with love         so softly, love.
```

Take My Breath Away (Love Theme)

from the Paramount Picture TOP GUN

Words and Music by Giorgio Moroder and Tom Whitlock

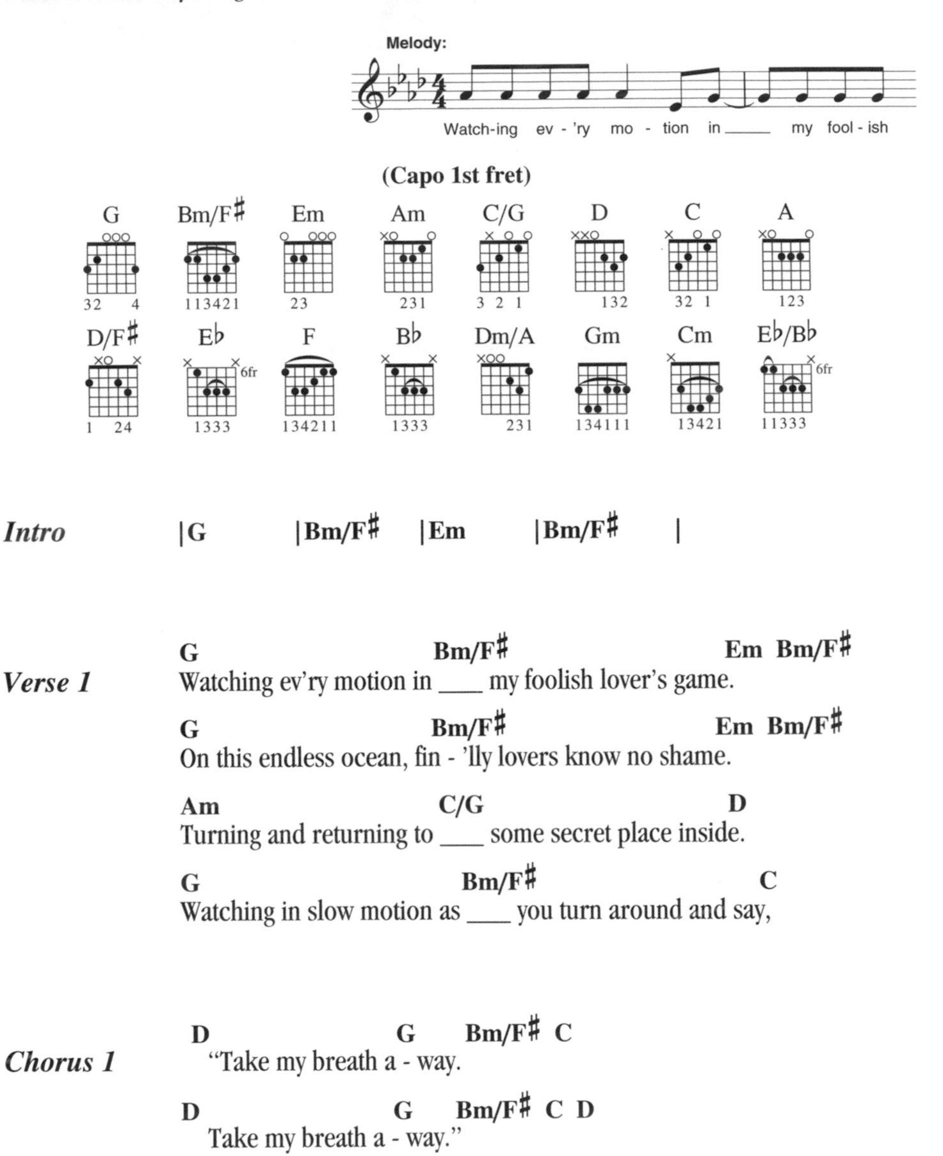

Verse 2

```
G                                   Bm/F#                 Em  Bm/F#
Watching, I keep waiting, still ___ anticipating love.
G                      Bm/F#                        Em  Bm/F#
Never hesitating to ___ become the fated ones.
Am                        C/G                       D
Turning and returning to ___ some secret place to hide.
G                                Bm/F#                       C
Watching in slow motion as ___ you turn to me and say,
```

Chorus 2

```
      D                    G       Bm/F#  Em  Bm/F#  G
"My love, take my breath a - way."
```

Bridge

```
A                                 D/F#
Through the hourglass I saw ___ you.
          C                   G
In time, ___ you slipped away.
A                                    D/F#
When the mirror crashed I called ___ you.
          C                 G
I turned ___ to hear you say,
                   A            D
"If only for to - day I am un - afraid.
```

Chorus 3

```
                     G       Bm/F#  Em
"Take my breath a - way.
Bm/F#                  G       Bm/F#  Em  Eb  F
    Take my breath a - way."
```

```
            Bb                    Dm/A                      Gm  Dm/A
Verse 3     Watching every motion in ___ this foolish lover's game.

            Bb                      Dm/A                        Gm  Dm/A
            Haunted by the notion some - where there's a love in flames.

            Cm                   Eb/Bb                     F
            Turning and returning to ___ some secret place inside.

            Bb                      Dm/A                Eb/Bb    F
            Watching in slow motion as ___ you turn my way, ___ and say,
```

```
                               Bb   Dm/A
Outro-Chorus  "Take my breath a - way.

               Eb           F                Bb   Dm/A
            ||:  My love, ___ take my breath a - way."   :||   Repeat and fade
```

Time in a Bottle

Words and Music by Jim Croce

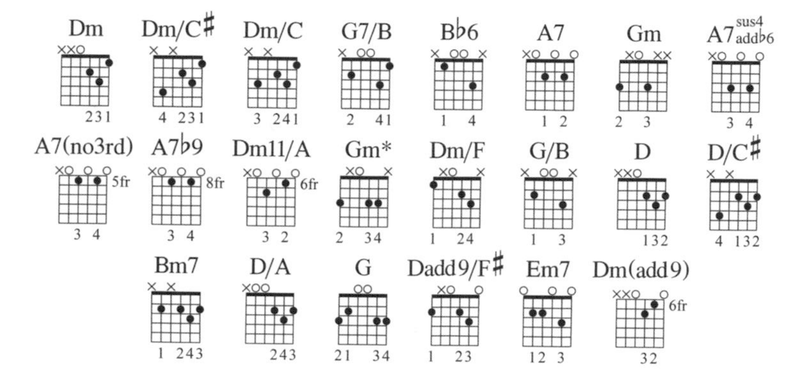

Intro

| **Dm** | **Dm/C♯** | **Dm/C** | **G7/B** |
| **B♭6** | **A7 Gm** | **A7 A7$^{\text{sus4}}_{\text{add}\flat 6}$ A7(no3rd)** |
| **A7♭9 Dm11/A A7(no3rd)** |

Verse 1

Dm Dm/C♯ Dm/C G7/B
If I could save ____ time in a bottle,

B♭6 A7 Gm
The first thing that I'd like to do

| **A7 A7$^{\text{sus4}}_{\text{add}\flat 6}$ A7(no3rd)** | **A7♭9 Dm11/A A7(no3rd)** |

Dm Dm/C
Is to save ev'ry-day

B♭6 Gm* Dm/F
Till e-ternity pass - es away

Gm* A7 G/B A7(no3rd) A7
Just to spend them with you.

Verse 2

```
  Dm            Dm/C#       Dm/C  G7/B
If I could make days last for-ever,
  Bb6                        A7  Gm
If words could make wish-es  come
A7  A7sus4/addb6  A7(no3rd)  A7b9  Dm11/A  A7(no3rd)
True;
    Dm        Dm/C
I'd save ev'ry-day
        Bb6         Gm*
Like a treasure and then,
   Dm/F       Gm*                  A7  G/B  A7(no3rd)  A7
A-gain I would spend them with you.
```

Chorus 1

```
                D                D/C#
But there never seems to be enough time
     Bm7               D/A                 G
To do the things you wanna do once you find them.
| Dadd9/F#      | Em7            | A7   G/B   A7(no3rd) |
      D                  D/C#
I've looked around e-nough to know
       Bm7              D/A                 G
That you're the one I want to go through time with.
| Dadd9/F#      | Em7            | A7   G/B   A7(no3rd) |
```

Interlude *Repeat Intro*

Verse 3

```
 Dm      Dm/C#      Dm/C G7/B
If I had a box just for wishes,

    Bb6                      A7  Gm
And dreams that had never __ come

A7 A7sus4/addb6 A7(no3rd) A7b9 Dm11/A A7(no3rd)
True;

    Dm           Dm/C
The box would be empty

   Bb6         Gm*          Dm/F
Ex-cept for the mem'ry of  how

          Gm*              A7 G/B A7(no3rd) A7
They were answered by you.
```

Chorus 2 *Repeat Chorus 1*

Outro ||: **Dm(add9)** | :|| *Play 3 times*

Through the Years

Words and Music by
Steve Dorff and Marty Panzer

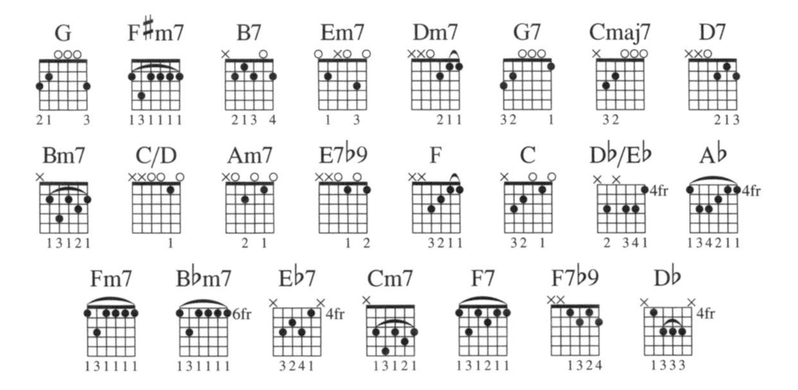

Verse 1

```
G                         F♯m7       B7          Em7
I can't remember when__ you were - n't there,

Dm7   G7        Cmaj7  D7            Bm7   C/D
When I didn't care__ for anyone but you,

G                              F♯m7       B7          Em7
I swear we've been through ev'rything __ there is,

               Dm7        G7          Cmaj7
Can't imagine anything ___ we've missed.

               G              Am7              C/D
Can't imagine anything the two of us can't do.
```

Chorus 1

```
              G
Through the years

        Em7           Am7
You've never let me down,

        C/D            D7  Bm7
You've turned my life__ a - round.

     Em7                Am7
The sweetest days I've found

                C/D
I've found with you.

D7           Bm7
Through the years,

    E7♭9         Am7
I've never been a-fraid,

    D7                 Bm7
I've loved the life we've made,

    E7♭9             Cmaj7
And I'm so glad I've stayed

           Bm7    Am7
Right here with you

C/D         G     Em7     F   C   C/D
Through the years.
```

Verse 2

```
 G                        F♯m7     B7      Em7
I can't remember what__ I used__ to do,

Dm7  G7         Cmaj7
Who I trusted, who

 D7             Bm7
I listened to be-fore.

 G                             F♯m7    B7        Em7
I swear you've taught me ev'rything __ I know,

                Dm7          G7        Cmaj7
Can't imagine needing some - one so.

                          G
But through the years it seems to me

 Am7                    C/D
I need you more and more.
```

Chorus 2

```
                G
Through the years,
            Em7                   Am7
Through all the good and bad,
C/D                 D7   Bm7
I knew how much__ we__ had.
     Em7                Am7                C/D
I've always been so glad to be with you.
D7              Bm7
Through the years,
    E7♭9        Am7
It's better ev'ry day.
        D7                    Bm7
You've kissed my tears a-way.
   E7♭9         Cmaj7
As long as it's o-kay
         Bm7     Am7
I'll stay with you
C/D            G      D♭/E♭
Through the years.
```

Chorus 3

```
                A♭
Through the years
          Fm7                 B♭m7
When ev - 'rything went wrong,
   D♭/E♭ E♭7      Cm7
To-gether we were strong.
  F7                      B♭m7
I know that I belonged
                         D♭/E♭
Right here with you.
E♭7            Cm7
Through the years
  F7♭9         B♭m7
I never had a doubt
            E♭7                Cm7
We'd al - ways work things out.
     F7♭9                         D♭
I've learned what love's about
   Cm7  B♭m7
By loving you
D♭/E♭        A♭
Through the years.
```

Chorus 4

```
             A♭
Through the years

      Fm7           B♭m7
You've never let me down,

      D♭/E♭         E♭7   Cm7
You've turned my life__ a - round.

    F7                      B♭m7
The sweetest days I've found

                      D♭/E♭
I've found with you.

E♭7          Cm7
Through the years,

   F7♭9
It's better ev'ry day;

      E♭7                  Cm7
You've kissed my tears a-way.

  F7♭9              D♭
As long as it's okay

   Cm7      B♭m7
I'll stay with you

D♭/E♭       A♭
Through the years.
```

A Time for Us (Love Theme)

from the Paramount Picture ROMEO AND JULIET

Words by Larry Kusik and Eddie Snyder
Music by Nino Rota

Intro

|Am |F/A |G/A |Am |

Verse 1

```
               Em          F
A time for us someday there'll be
               C                        Dm                  Am
When chains are torn by courage born of a love that's free.
               Em                        F          Dm    E
A time when dreams so long de - nied can flour - ish
   Am                             Em      Am
As we unveil the love we now must hide.
```

Bridge 1

```
  C         G      Dm     Am
A time for us at last to see
  B♭         F          Em        Am
A life worth - while for you and me.
```

Verse 2

```
               Em                       F
And with our love through tears and thorns

              C                Dm                 Am
We will en - dure as we pass surely through ev'ry storm.

           Em                 F    Dm  E
A time for us someday there'll be a new world,

  Am                          Em  Am
A world of shining hope for you and  me.
```

Bridge 2

Repeat Bridge 1

Verse 3

```
               Em                 F
And with our love through tears and thorns

              C                Dm                 Am
We will en - dure as we pass surely through ev'ry storm.

           Em                 F    Dm  E
A time for us someday there'll be a new world,

  Am                          Em  Am  Em  A
A world of shining hope for you and  me.
```

Unchained Melody

from the Motion Picture UNCHAINED

Lyric by Hy Zaret
Music by Alex North

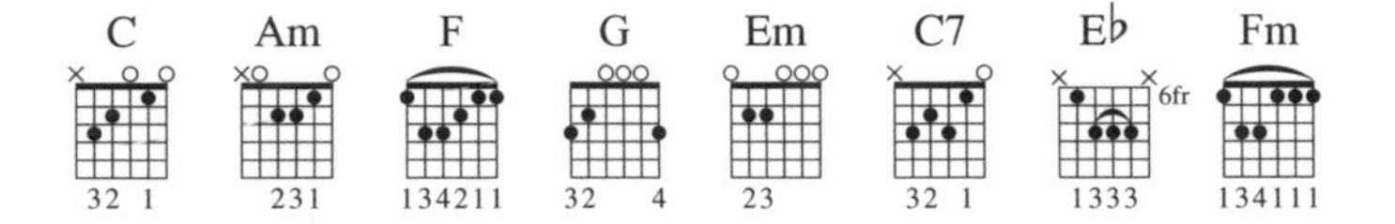

Verse 1

C **Am** **F**
Whoa, my ___ love, my ___ darlin',

G **C** **Am** **G**
I've hungered for your ___ touch, a long lonely time.

C **Am** **F**
And time goes ___ by so ___ slowly

G **C**
And time can do so ___ much.

Am **G**
Are ___ you still mine?

C **G** **Am** **Em**
I ___ need your love. I need ___ your love.

F **G** **C** **C7**
God speed your love to me.

Bridge

F G F E♭
Lonely rivers flow to the sea, to the sea,

F G C
To the open arms of the sea, yeah.

F G F E♭
Lonely rivers sigh, "Wait for me, wait for me.

F G C
I'll be comin' home, wait for me."

Verse 2

C Am F
Whoa, my ___ love, my ___ darlin',

G C Am G
I've hungered, hungered for your ___ touch, a long lonely time.

C Am F
And time goes ___ by so ___ slowly

G C
And time can do so ___ much.

Am G
Are ___ you still mine?

C G Am Em
I ___ need your ___ love. I ___ need ___ your love.

F G C Am F Fm C
God speed your love to me.

Up Where We Belong

from the Paramount Picture
AN OFFICER AND A GENTLEMAN

Words by Will Jennings
Music by Buffy Sainte-Marie and Jack Nitzsche

Melody:

Who knows what _ to - mor-row brings, _

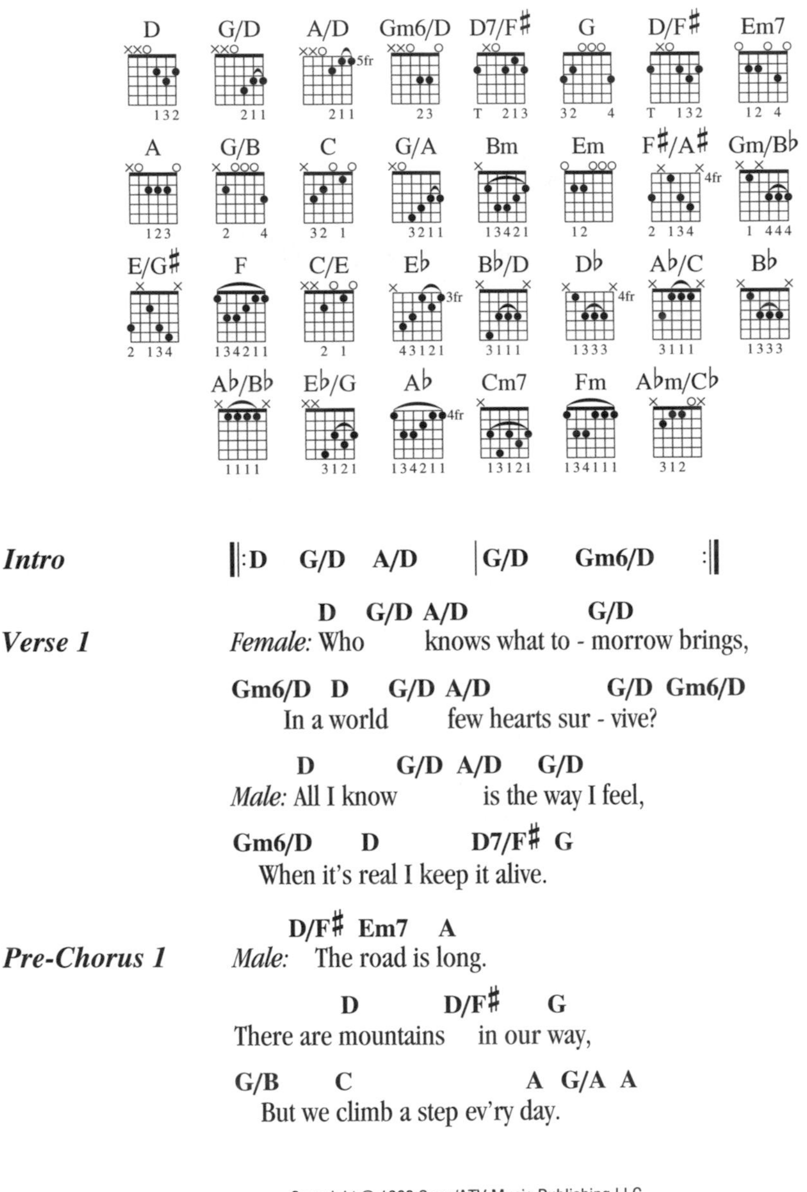

Intro

‖: D G/D A/D | G/D Gm6/D :‖

Verse 1

D G/D A/D G/D
Female: Who knows what to - morrow brings,

Gm6/D D G/D A/D G/D Gm6/D
In a world few hearts sur - vive?

D G/D A/D G/D
Male: All I know is the way I feel,

Gm6/D D D7/F♯ G
When it's real I keep it alive.

Pre-Chorus 1

D/F♯ Em7 A
Male: The road is long.

D D/F♯ G
There are mountains in our way,

G/B C A G/A A
But we climb a step ev'ry day.

```
                         D             D/F♯                 G
Chorus 1        Both:   Love lift us up where we belong,

                Bm         Em          D/F♯   C         G   A
                Where the eagles cry    on a mountain high.

                D              D/F♯                 G
                  Love lift us up where we belong,

                Bm              Em          D/F♯
                Far from the world below,

                             F♯/A♯      Bm  Gm/B♭  D  G/D  A/D  G/D  Gm6/D
                Up where the clear winds blow.

                      D    G/D  A/D          G/D
Verse 2         Male: Some          hang on to "used to be,'

                Gm6/D     D   G/D  A/D          G/D  Gm6/D
                  Live their lives         lookin' be - hind.

                          D         G/D  A/D  G/D
                Female: All we have          is here and now,

                Gm6/D   D       D7/F♯    G
                  All our life, out there to find.


Pre-Chorus 2    Repeat Pre-Chorus 1

                         D             D/F♯                 G
Chorus 2        Both:   Love lift us up where we belong,

                Bm             Em        D/F♯   C          G   A
                  Where the eagles cry    on a mountain high.

                D              D/F♯                G
                  Love lift us up where we belong,

                Bm              Em             D/F♯
                Far from the world we know,

                         E/G♯      G/A
                Where the clear winds blow.
```

```
              F                   C/E  Eb              Bb/D
Bridge          Time goes by,         no time to cry.

              Db              Ab/C  Bb       Ab/Bb  Bb
              Life's you and I, a  -  live, to - day.

                          Eb             Eb/G                 Ab
Chorus 3      Both: ||:  Love lift us up where we belong,

              Cm7           Fm         Eb/G    Db             Ab/C  Bb
                Where the eagles cry      on a mountain high.

              Eb             Eb/G                Ab
                Love lift us up where we belong,

              Cm7          Fm              Eb/G
              Far from the world we know,

                          G/B          Cm7   Abm/Cb
              Where the clear winds blow.            :||  Repeat and fade
```

Vision of Love

Words and Music by Mariah Carey and Ben Margulies

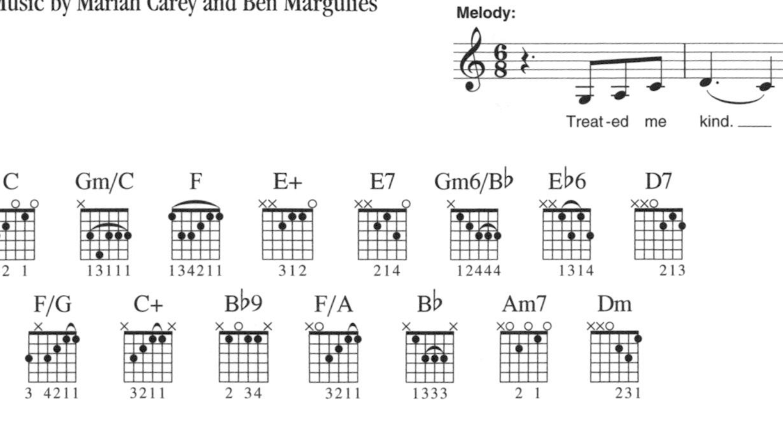

Verse 1

N.C. C
Treated me kind.

Gm/C F
Sweet desti - ny carried me through desperation

E+ E7
To the one that was waiting for me.

C Gm6/B♭
It took so long, still I believed

F E+ E7
Somehow the one that I needed would find me e - ventually.

Chorus 1

E♭6 D7
I had a vision of love,

F F/G C C+
And it was all that you've given to me.

```
              C  Bb9  N.C.                    C                    Gm/C
Verse 2                  Prayed through the nights, felt so a - lone.

                       F          E+                  E7
              Suffered from alienation,    carried the weight on my own.

              C                   Gm6/Bb
                Had to be strong,     so I believed,

              F                                   E+                E7
                And now I know I've succeeded    in finding the place I conceived.


              Eb6        D7
Chorus 2        I had a vision of love,

              F               F/G                       Eb6
                And it was all that you've given to me.

                    D7
              I had a vision of love,

              F               F/G  N.C.              F/A
                And it was all    that you've giv - en me.


              Bb                    C       Am7
Bridge          I've realized a dream,     mm,

              Bb                          C                      Am7
                And I visualized the love that came to be.

              Bb                          C                          Am7
                Feel so alive. I'm so thankful that I've re - ceived

                  Dm                          F/G
              The answer that heaven has sent down to me.
```

Verse 3

```
N.C.              C           Gm6/B♭
   You treated me kind, sweet ___ destiny, yes,

F                               E+            E7
   And I'll be eternally grateful   holding you so close to me.

C                              Gm6/B♭
   Prayed through the nights    so faithfully,

F                                  E+                    E7
   Knowing the one that I needed    would find me e - ventually.
```

Chorus 3

```
E♭6      D7
   I had a vision of love,

F             F/G                     E♭6
   And it was all that you've given to me.

      D7
I had a vision of love,

F             F/G  E♭6  D7  F  N.C.                     C  C+  C  C+
   And it was all                    that you turned out to be.

C  B♭9   C
   Yeah. Mm.
```

Valentine

Words and Music by Jack Kugell
and Jim Brickman

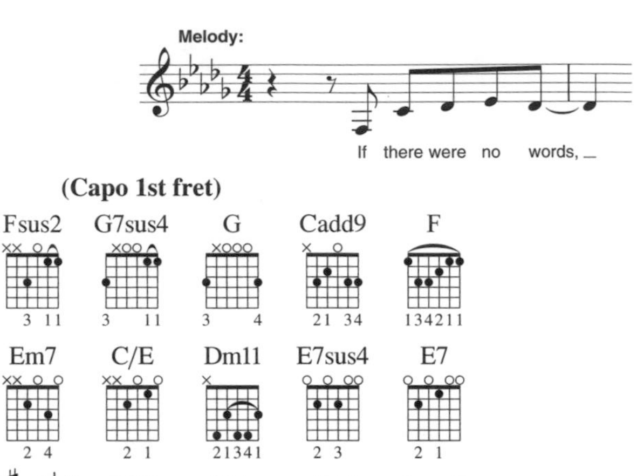

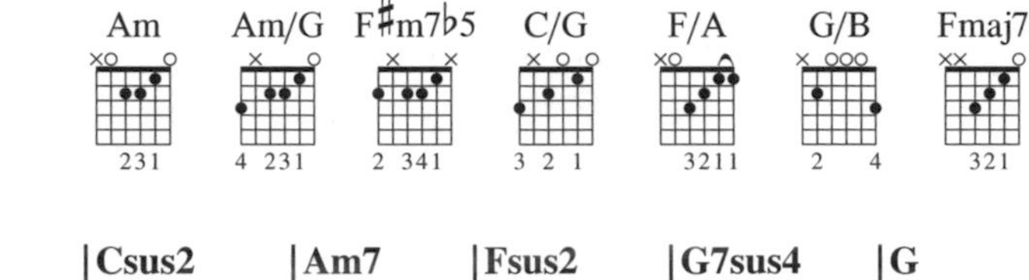

Intro | **Csus2** | **Am7** | **Fsus2** | **G7sus4** | **G** |

Verse 1

Cadd9 Am7 F
If there were no words, ___ no way to speak,
Gsus4 G Cadd9
I ___ would still ___ hear you.
Am7 F
If there were no tears, ___ no way to feel ___ inside,
F/G
I'd still ___ feel for you.

Chorus 1

Em7 C/E F G Em7
And even if the sun ___ refused ___ to shine,
C/E F G Dm11
E - ven if romance ___ ran out ___ of rhyme,
E7sus4 E7 Am Am/G F♯m7♭5
You would still have my heart until ___ the end ___ of time.
C/G G7sus4 Csus2 Am7 Fsus2 G7sus4 G
You're all I need, my love, ___ my valentine.

```
                Cadd9          Am7                      F
Verse 2           All of my life, ___ I have been wait - ing

                     Gsus4          G          Cadd9
                For all ___ you give ___ to me.

                                       Am7
                You've opened my eyes

                                     F                F/G
                And shown me how ___ to love unself - ishly.


                    Em7        C/E        F            G          Em7
Chorus 2        I've dreamed of this a thou - sand times ___ before,

                  C/E                F          G        Dm11
                In my dreams I could - n't love ___ you more.

                     E7sus4     E7        Am         Am/G       F#m7b5
                I will give you my heart until ___ the end ___ of time.

                      C/G                 G7sus4
                You're all I need, my love, ___ my valentine.


Bridge          |Cadd9         |Am7        |F          | F/A     G/B       |
                                                    La, la,  la, la, la, ___ la, la.
                |Cadd9         |Am7        |F          |Gsus4    G         |


                    Em7  C/E        F            G          Em7
Chorus 3        And even  if the sun ___ refused ___ to shine,

                   C/E                 F           G     Dm11
                E - ven if romance ___ ran out ___ of rhyme,

                          E7sus4      E7         Am          Am/G       F#m7b5
                You would still have my heart until ___ the end ___ of time.

                      C/G             G7sus4          Dm11
                'Cause all I need is you, ___ my valentine.

                    C/E      Fmaj7  C/G              G7sus4            Csus2
                Oh, ___ oh.   You're all I need, my love, ___ my valentine.

                Am7  F   G7sus4  Cadd9
                  Oh, oh.
```

The Way We Were

from the Motion Picture THE WAY WE WERE

Words by Alan and Marilyn Bergman
Music by Marvin Hamlisch

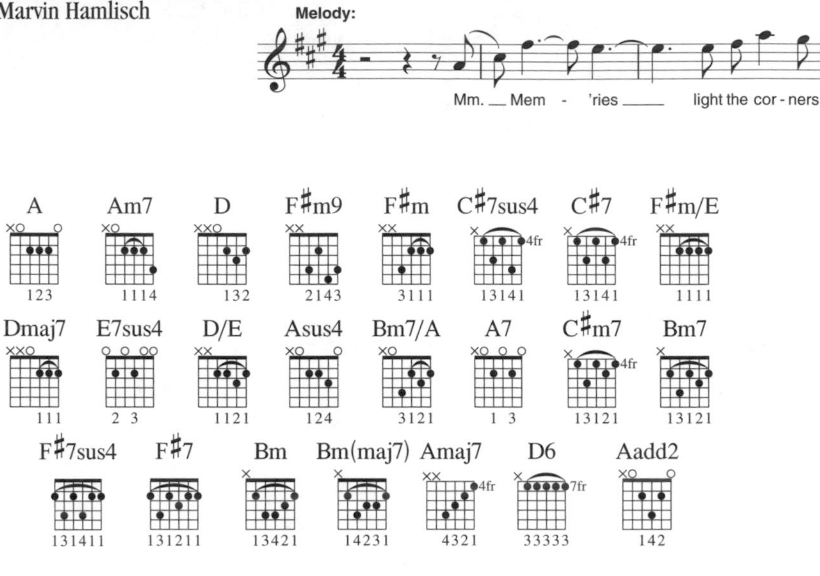

Intro |**A** |

Verse 1 |**A Amaj7** |**D** |**F♯m9 F♯m** |**D C♯7sus4 C♯7** |
w/ vocal humming throughout.
|**F♯m F♯m/E** |**Dmaj7 E7sus4** |**A** |**D D/E** |

Verse 2
A Asus4 F♯m F♯m/E
Mem'ries ___ light the corners ___ of my mind.
Dmaj7 C♯7sus4 C♯7 F♯m F♯m/E
Misty water - color mem'ries
Dmaj7 E7sus4 A Bm7/A D/E
Of the way we were.

Verse 3

```
A                  Asus4              F#m          F#m/E
  Scattered pictures ___ of the smiles we ___ left behind,
Dmaj7  C#7sus4  C#7       F#m  F#m/E
       Smiles we gave to one another
Dmaj7  E7sus4          A   A7
         For the way we were.
```

Bridge

```
Dmaj7                 C#m7  Bm7
  Can it be that it was all _______ so simple then,
C#m7                        F#7sus4  F#7
  Or has time rewritten ev - 'ry line?
Bm      Bm(maj7)                  E7sus4
  If we had the chance to do it all again,
       Amaj7      D6/E
Tell me would we?       Could we?
```

Verse 4

```
A         Asus4                    F#m  F#m/E
Mem'ries ___ may be beautiful, and yet,
Dmaj7  C#7sus4  C#7      F#m          F#m/E
  What's too      painful to ___ remember
Dmaj7 C#7sus4      C#7    F#m       F#m/E
  We sim - ply choose ___ to ___ forget.
Dmaj7       C#m7  Dmaj7        C#m7
  So it's the laughter ____ we will remember,
Dmaj7             C#m7
  Whenever we re - member
Bm7  D/E     A        Asus4             A
       The way we were.    The way we were.
```

Outro

```
|A     |Asus4   |C#m7    |Dmaj7   |A(add2)  ||
```

We've Only Just Begun

Words and Music by
Roger Nichols and Paul Williams

Melody:

We've on - ly just be-gun ___

A Dmaj7 C♯m7 F♯m7 Bm7 E7sus4 E7

Amaj7 E F♯ Bmaj7 B♭ E♭maj7 C♯

Intro | A | Dmaj7 | A | Dmaj7 |

Verse 1

A Dmaj7 C♯m7
We've only just be - gun to live,

F♯m7 Bm7
White lace and ___ promises,

F♯m7 Bm7 E7sus4 E7
A kiss for luck and we're on our way.

Verse 2

A Dmaj7 C♯m7
Before the rising sun we ______ fly.

F♯m7 Bm7
So many roads to choose,

F♯m7 Bm7 E7sus4
We start out walking and learn to run.

Amaj7 Dmaj7 Amaj7 Dmaj7 E
(And, yes, we've just be - gun.)

Bridge 1

F♯ Bmaj7 F♯ Bmaj7
Sharing ho - rizons that are new to us,

F♯ Bmaj7 F♯ Bmaj7
Watching the signs ___ along the way.

B♭ E♭maj7 B♭ E♭maj7
Talking it over, just the two of us,

B♭ E♭maj7 E7sus4 E7
Working to - gether day to day, to - gether.

Verse 3

A **Dmaj7** **C#m7**
And when the evening comes we smile,

F#m7 **Bm7**
So much of life ahead,

F#m7 **Bm7** **E7sus4**
We'll find a place where there's room to grow.

Amaj7 **Dmaj7** **Amaj7** **Dmaj7** **E**
(And, yes, we've just be - gun.)

Bridge 2

F# **Bmaj7** **F#** **Bmaj7**
Sharing ho - rizons that are new to us,

F# **Bmaj7** **F#** **Bmaj7**
Watching the signs ___ along the way.

Bb **Ebmaj7** **Bb** **Ebmaj7**
Talking it over, just the two of us,

Bb **Ebmaj7** **E7sus4** **E7** **N.C.**
Working to - gether day to day, to - gether, together.

Verse 4

A **Dmaj7** **C#m7**
And when the evening comes we smile,

F#m7 **Bm7**
So much of life ahead,

F#m7 **Bm7** **E7sus4**
We'll find a place where there's room to grow.

Amaj7 **Dmaj7** **Amaj7** **Dmaj7** **C#**
And, yes, we've just be - gun.

What the World Needs Now Is Love

Lyric by Hal David
Music by Burt Bacharach

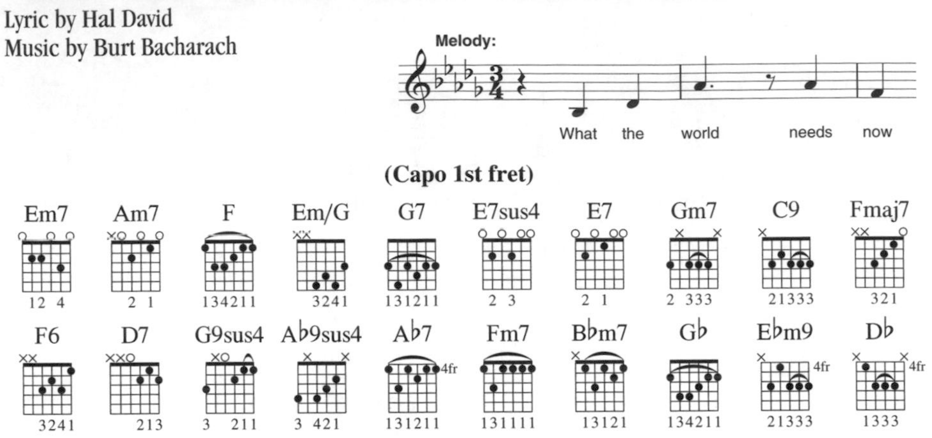

Intro

‖: **Em7** | **Am7** :‖

Chorus 1

```
                Em7           Am7   Em7         Am7
What the world needs now is love, sweet love.
F                               Em/G  G7
It's the only thing that there's just too little of.
                Em7           Am7   Em7         Am7
What the world needs now is love, sweet love.
F                               E7sus4  E7
No, not just for some, but for ev'ryone.
```

Verse 1

Am7
Lord, we don't need another mountain.

Gm7 C9 Fmaj7 F6
There are mountains and hillsides e - nough to climb.

Gm7 C9 Fmaj7
There are oceans and rivers e - nough to cross,

Am7 D7 G9sus4
E - nough to last till the end of time.

Chorus 2 *Repeat Chorus 1*

Verse 2

Am7
Lord, we don't need another meadow.

Gm7 C9 Fmaj7 F6
There are cornfields and wheatfields e - nough to grow.

Gm7 C9 Fmaj7
There are sunbeams and moonbeams e - nough to shine,

Am7 D7 G9sus4 G7 A♭9sus4 A♭7
Oh, listen, Lord, if you want to know.

Chorus 3

Fm7 B♭m7 Fm7 B♭m7
What the world needs now is love, sweet love.

G♭ Fm/A♭ A♭7
It's the only thing that there's just too little of.

Fm7 B♭m7 Fm7 B♭m7
What the world needs now is love, sweet love.

G♭ Fm7 B♭m7 E♭m9 A♭9sus4
No, not just for some, oh, but just for ev'ry, ev - 'ry,

D♭
Ev'ry - one.

Outro

| Fm7 | B♭m7 | Fm7 | B♭m7 |

Fm7 B♭m7 Fm7 B♭m7
||: (What the world needs now is love, sweet love.) :|| ***Play 3 times***

||: Fm7 | B♭m7 | Fm7 | B♭m7 :|| ***Repeat and fade***

Where Do I Begin (Love Theme)

from the Paramount Picture LOVE STORY

Words by Carl Sigman
Music by Francis Lai

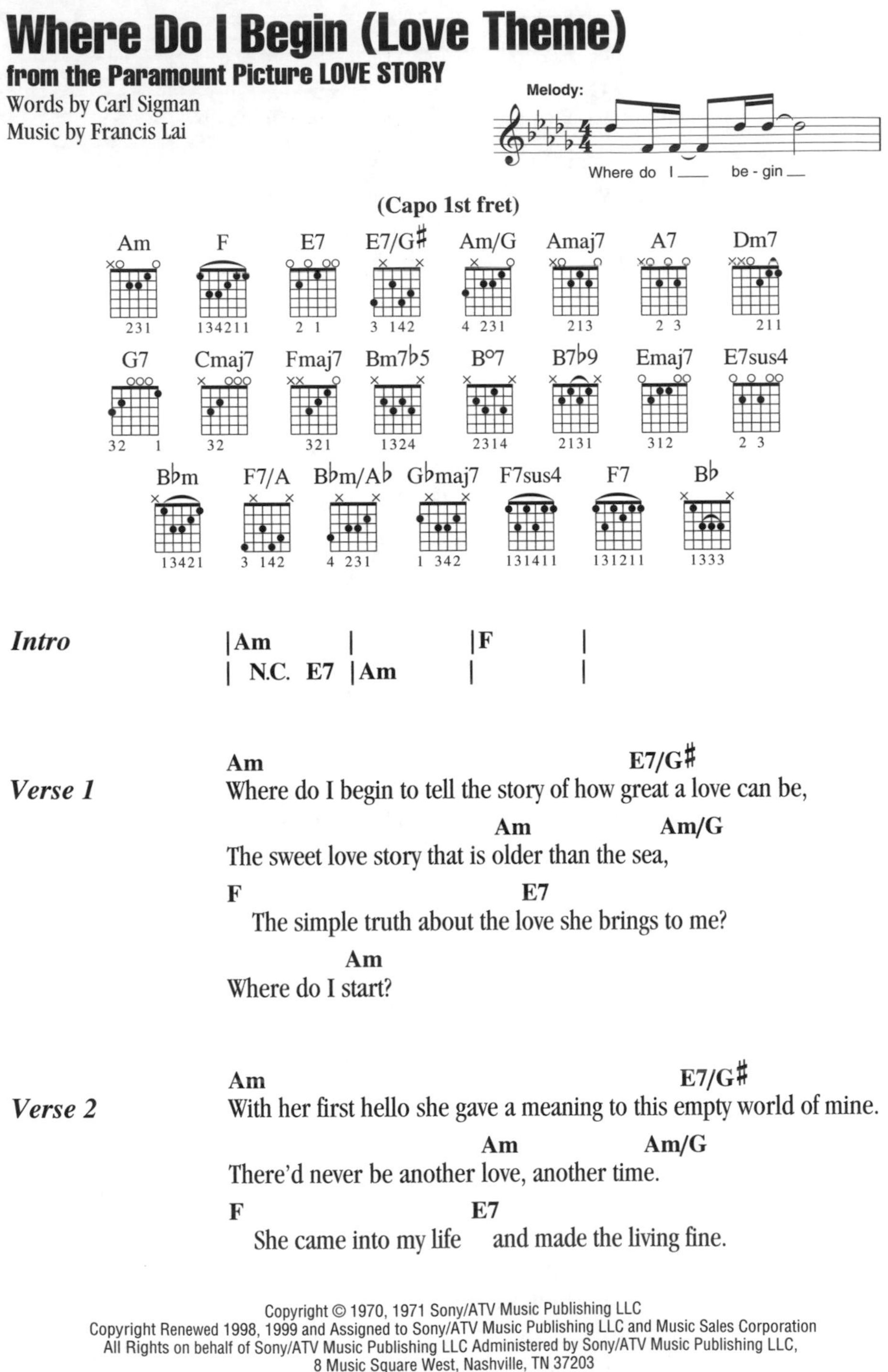

(Capo 1st fret)

Intro

Am		**F**	
N.C. E7	**Am**		

Verse 1

Am **E7/G♯**
Where do I begin to tell the story of how great a love can be,
Am **Am/G**
The sweet love story that is older than the sea,
F **E7**
The simple truth about the love she brings to me?
Am
Where do I start?

Verse 2

Am **E7/G♯**
With her first hello she gave a meaning to this empty world of mine.
Am **Am/G**
There'd never be another love, another time.
F **E7**
She came into my life and made the living fine.

```
                Amaj7
Bridge      She fills my heart.

            A7          Dm7          G7
              She fills my heart with very special things,

                  Cmaj7              Fmaj7
            With angel songs, with wild i - maginings.

                 Bm7b5  B°7             Am
            She fills my soul ___ with so much love

                        Dm7       G7
            That anywhere I go I'm never lonely.

                  Cmaj7            Fmaj7
            With her a - long, who could be lonely?

                        B7b9          Emaj7  E7
            I reach for her hand, it's always there.


            Am
Verse 3     How long does it last?

                                         E7/G#
            Can love be measured by the hours in a day?

                                         Am          Am/G
            I have no answers now, but this much I can say;

            Fmaj7                        E7sus4      E7
              I know I'll need her till the stars all burn a - way,

                        Am
            And she'll be there.


            Bbm
Verse 4       How long does it last?

                                         F7/A
            Can love be measured by the hours in a day?

                                         Bbm          Bbm/Ab
            I have no answers now, but this much I can say;

            Gbmaj7                       F7sus4      F7
              I know I'll need her till the stars all burn a - way,

                        Bbm  Bb
            And she'll be there.
```

Years from Now

Words and Music by Roger Cook
and Charles Cochran

(Capo 1st fret)

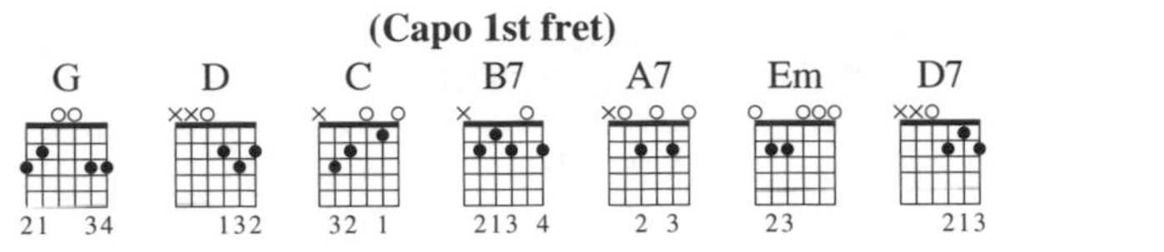

Intro ‖: G | D | C | D :‖

Verse 1

G D C
Years from now,

D G D C
I'll want you years from now,

D G B7 C
And I'll hold you years from now

A7 D D7
As I love you to - night.

Verse 2

G D C
You are my one true friend,

D G D C
Always my one true friend,

D G B7 C
And I'll love you till life's end

A7 D D7
As I love you to - night.

Bridge 1

```
C                         D
I know this world that we live in
                        G
Can be hard now and then,
      B7        Em
And it will be again.
      A7                D
Many times we've been down.
C                       D
Still love has kept us to - gether,
                    G
The flame never dies.
       B7              Em
When I look in your eyes,
    A7      D
The future I see.
```

Verse 3

```
             G     D    C
Wanting you years from now,
    D           G     D    C
And holding you years from now,
    D          G     B7   C
And loving you years from now
    D           G      D  C  D
As I love you to - night.
```

Guitar Solo

```
|G         |D          |C          |D           |
|G         |B7         |C          |A7          |
|D         |           |D7         |            |
```

Bridge 2 *Repeat Bridge 1*

Verse 4 *Repeat Verse 3*

Outro-Guitar Solo

```
     G     D    C     D
||: (Years from now.
 G     B7  C     D
 Years from now.)   :||  Repeat and fade
```

You Are So Beautiful

Words and Music by Billy Preston and Bruce Fisher

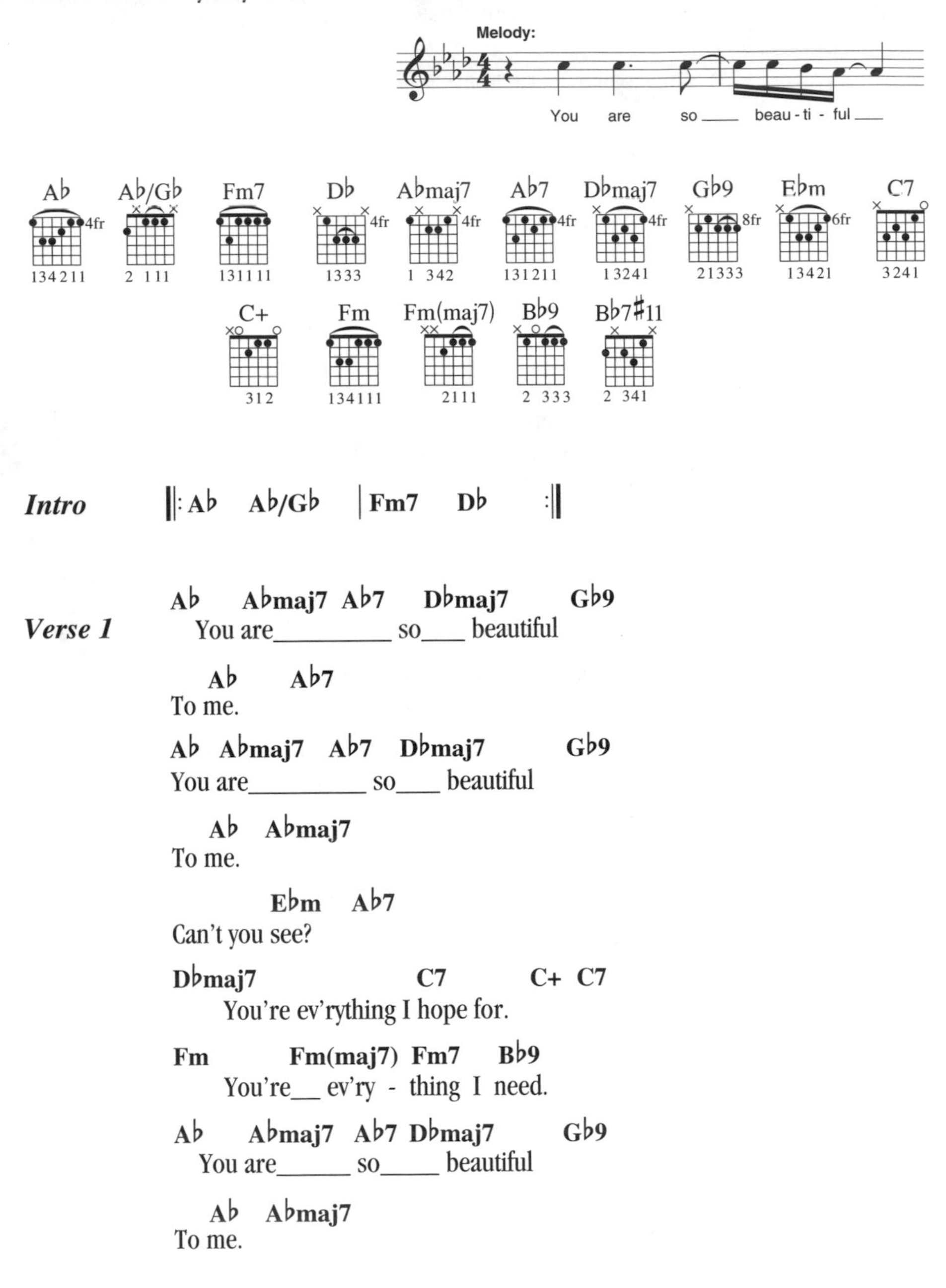

Intro ‖: **Ab Ab/Gb** | **Fm7 Db** :‖

Verse 1

Ab Abmaj7 Ab7 Dbmaj7 Gb9
You are_________ so___ beautiful

Ab Ab7
To me.

Ab Abmaj7 Ab7 Dbmaj7 Gb9
You are_________ so___ beautiful

Ab Abmaj7
To me.

Ebm Ab7
Can't you see?

Dbmaj7 C7 C+ C7
You're ev'rything I hope for.

Fm Fm(maj7) Fm7 Bb9
You're__ ev'ry - thing I need.

Ab Abmaj7 Ab7 Dbmaj7 Gb9
You are______ so_____ beautiful

Ab Abmaj7
To me.

Verse 2

Ab Abmaj7 Ab7 Dbmaj7 Gb9
You are_________ so___ beautiful

Ab Ab7
To me.

Ab Abmaj7 Ab7 Dbmaj7 Gb9
You are_________ so___ beautiful

Ab Abmaj7
To me.

Ebm Ab7
Can't you see?

Dbmaj7 C7 C+ C7
You're ev'rything I hope for.

Fm Bb7#11
Ev'rything I need.

Ab Abmaj7 Ab7 Dbmaj7 Gb9
You are_________ so___ beautiful

Ab Abmaj7 Ab7 Dbmaj7 Gb9 Ab
To__ me.

You Light Up My Life

Words and Music by
Joseph Brooks

Am D G Em F♯m7 B7 E7 D/F♯ F♯ A7

Dmaj7 D7 Em7 A/C♯ Bm E D/A Dsus4/A A

Intro | Am | |

Verse 1

Am D G Em
So many nights I'd sit by my window

F♯m7 B7 Em E7
Waiting for someone to sing me his song.

Am D G D/F♯ Em
So many dreams I kept deep ___ in - side me,

F♯ A7
A - lone in the dark, but now you've come along.

Chorus 1

D Dmaj7 D7
And you light up my life.

B7 Em
You give me hope to carry on.

Em7 A7
You light up my days

D A/C♯ Bm Em A7
And fill my nights ________ with ___ song.

Verse 2

```
Am        D        G            Em
Rollin' at sea, a - drift on the water,

F#m7      B7         Em          E7
Could it be fin'lly I'm turning for home?

Am      D            G          D/F# Em
Fin'lly a chance to say, "Hey! ___ I love you."

F#               A7
Never again to be all alone.
```

Chorus 2

Repeat Chorus 1

Outro-Chorus

```
         D          Dmaj7     D7
'Cause you, you light up my life.

                B7             Em
You give me hope to carry on.

     Em7         A7
You light up my days

              F#           Bm
And fill my nights with song.

E           D              F#          Bm
It can't be wrong when it feels so right,

E          D/A  Dsus4/A  A
   'Cause you

     G    D  A  G  D
You light up my life.
```

You Raise Me Up

Words and Music by
Brendan Graham and
Rolf Lovland

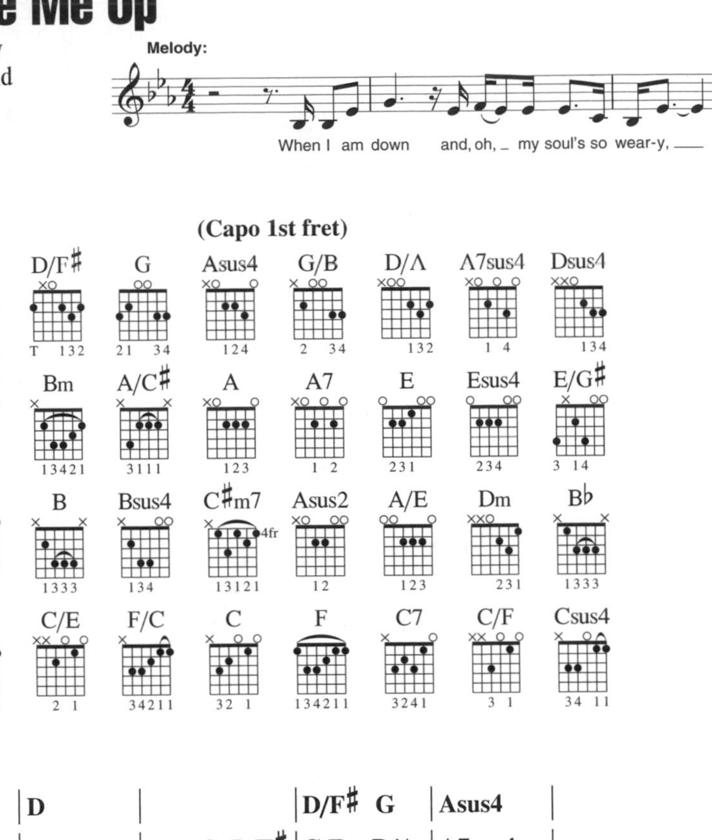

Intro

| D | | D/F♯ G | Asus4 |
| G/B | D/A G D/F♯ | G/B D/A | A7sus4 |
| D |

Verse

```
D                          Dsus4            D
   When I am down and, oh, my soul's so weary,
                  D/F♯     G                      Asus4
When troubles come and my heart burdened be,
             G                          D/F♯
Then I am still and wait here in the silence
G            D            A7/D           D
   Until you come and sit a while with me.
```

Chorus 1

```
          Bm       G            D/F♯
You raise me up so I can stand on mountains.
A/C♯          Bm  G              D/F♯
  You raise me up to walk on stormy seas.
A      D          G/B          D/A   D/F♯
  I am strong when I am on your shoul - ders.
G              D/A  A7            D
  You raise me up to more than I can be.
```

Interlude

```
| E   Esus4 | E         | E/G♯  A  | E/B   B |
| A/C♯  A   | E/G♯  A   | E/B Bsus4 | E      |
```

Chorus 2

```
            C♯m7  A           E/G♯
You raise me up so  I can stand on mountains.
B              C♯m7  A            E/B
  You raise me up to  walk on stormy seas.
B      E
  I am strong when I am on your shoulders.
Asus2          E/B  Bsus4          E     A/E  E
  You raise me up to more than I can ___ be.
```

Chorus 3

```
N.C.        Dm   B♭           F/A
You raise me up so I can stand on mountains.
C/E            Dm  B♭           F/C
  You raise me up to walk on stormy seas.
C      F          B♭          F
  I am strong when I am on your shoulders.
B♭             F/C  C7            F
  You raise me up to more than I can be.
```

Outro-Chorus

```
A7             Dm   B♭          F/A
  You raise me up so I can stand on mountains.
C/E            Dm  B♭           F/C
  You raise me up to walk on stormy seas.
C      F          C/F         F
  I am strong when I am on your shoulders.
B♭             F/C  Csus4          Dm  B♭
  You raise me up to more than I can be.
N.C.         F/C  C7             B♭     C/F  F
You raise me up to more than I can ___ be.
```

You've Got a Friend

Words and Music by Carole King

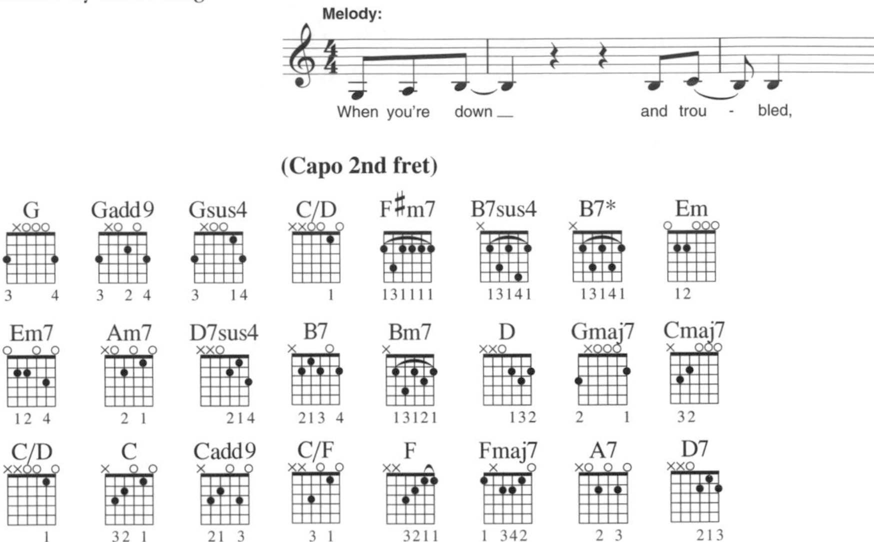

Intro | **G Gadd9 Gsus4** | **C/D** | **Gsus4 G Gadd9 G** | **F♯m7 B7sus4**

Verse 1

```
         B7*        Em         B7
When you're down__ and trou - bled,

          Em      B7              Em  Em7
And you need a helping hand,

    Am7           D7sus4                G   Gsus4 G Gsus4 G
And nothing, whoa, nothing is goin' right,

F♯m7                 B7
Close your eyes and think of me,

    Em       B7           Em  Em7
And soon I will__ be there

   Am7        Bm7                     D7sus4  D
To brighten up even your darkest night.
```

Chorus 1

G Gmaj7
You just call__ out my name,

Cmaj7 Am7
And you know wherever I am

D7sus4 G Gmaj7
I'll come run - ning, oh yeah, babe,

D7sus4
To see you again.

G Gmaj7
Winter, spring, summer or fall,

Cmaj7 Em7
Now, all you got to do is call,

Cmaj7 Bm7 C/D D7sus4
And I'll be there,__ yeah, yeah, yeah.

G Gadd9 G C G F♯m7 B7sus4
You've got a friend.

Verse 2

B7 Em B7
If the sky__ above__ you

Em B7 Em Em7
Should turn__ dark and full of clouds,

Am7 D7sus4 G Gsus4 G
And that old North wind should begin to blow,

F♯m7 B7
Keep your head togeth - er

Em B7 Em Em7 Am7
And call my name__ out loud, now.

Bm7 D7sus4
Soon I'll be knock - in' upon your door.

Chorus 2

Cadd9   Gmaj7
You just call__ out my name,

Cmaj7   Am7
And you know__ wherever I am,

D7sus4   G   Gsus4   G
I'll come run - ning,   oh yes, I will,

D7sus4
To see you again.

G   Gmaj7
Winter, spring, summer or fall,

Cmaj7   Em7
Yeah, all you got to do is call,

Cmaj7   Bm7   C/D D7sus4
And I'll be there, yeah,__ yeah, yeah.

Bridge

C/F   F
Hey, ain't__ it good to know

C/D
That you've got a friend

G   Gsus4   Gmaj7
When people can be__ so cold?

C
They'll hurt you,

Fmaj7
And desert you.

Em   Em7   A7
Well, they'll take your soul if you let__ them,

D7sus4   D7
Oh yeah, but don't__ you let them.

```
                     Gmaj7
*Chorus 3*  You just call__ out my name,

                Cmaj7                  Am7
            And you know wherever I am,

            D7sus4          G          Gsus4  G
               I'll come run-ning

                                D7sus4
            To see you again.

            Oh, babe, don't you know 'bout

            G                               Gmaj7
            Winter, spring, summer or fall,

                   Cmaj7                      Em7
            Hey, now all you've got to do is call.

                    Cmaj7          Bm7     C/D  D7sus4
            Lord, I'll be__ there, yes, I will.


                                 G  Gadd9 G  C
*Outro*     You've got a friend.

                          G
            You've got a friend, yeah.

            C                                  G
                 Ain't it good to know you've got__ a friend?

                 C
            Ain't it good to know

                                Gsus4  G  Gadd9  G
            You've got a friend?

                C                                 Gsus4 G Gadd9 G
            Oh,__ yeah, yeah. You've got a friend.
```